D1590731

The Magic Presence

BELOVED SAINT GERMAIN'S TALKS

"I AM" ACTIVITY
OF
SAINT GERMAIN FOUNDATION

The "I AM" Activity represents the Original, Permanent, and Highest Source of the Ascended Masters' Instruction on the Great Laws of Life, as first offered to the western world by the Ascended Master Saint Germain, through His Accredited Messengers, Mr. and Mrs. Guy W. Ballard.

In the early 1930s the Ballards established Saint Germain Foundation and Saint Germain Press, Inc., which under Saint Germain's Guidance, have expanded into worldwide organizations that offer to mankind the true Ascended Master Teachings on the Great Cosmic Words, "I AM"! Saint Germain Foundation strives to keep the "I AM" Ascended Master Instruction in Its pure, unadulterated form, free from any human interpretation, personal monetary gain, or proselytizing, as It is a Gift from the Great Ascended Masters and Cosmic Beings to bring Illumination and Perfection to mankind.

Hundreds of "I AM" Temples and Sanctuaries exist throughout the world, where the Teachings are applied in "I AM" Decree Groups. The Books of the Saint Germain Series are available in many libraries, bookstores, or directly from Saint Germain Press (address below). For further information, please contact:

SAINT GERMAIN FOUNDATION
SAINT GERMAIN PRESS
1120 Stonehedge Drive
Schaumburg, Illinois 60194 USA
(847) 882-7400 or (800) 662-2800
www.SaintGermainFoundation.org
www.SaintGermainPress.org

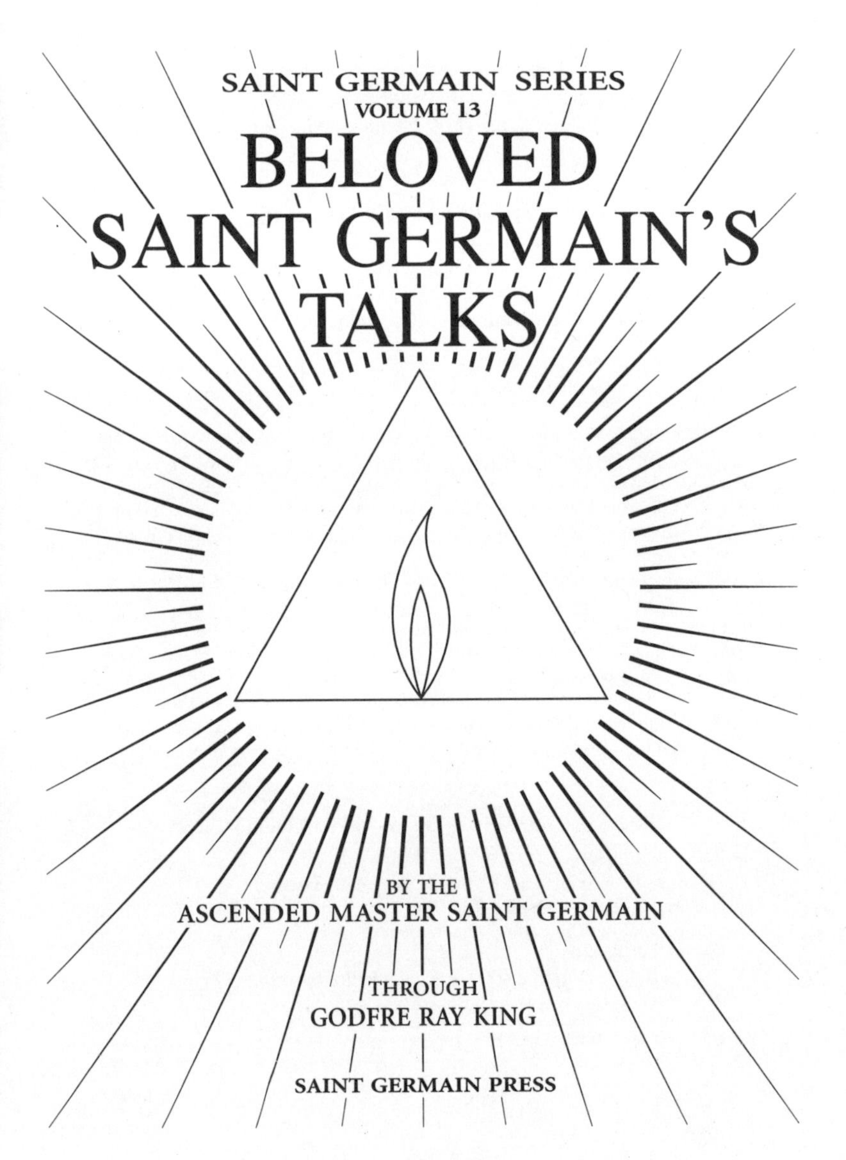

SAINT GERMAIN SERIES
VOLUME 13

BELOVED SAINT GERMAIN'S TALKS

BY THE
ASCENDED MASTER SAINT GERMAIN

THROUGH
GODFRE RAY KING

SAINT GERMAIN PRESS

2000 Printing
Printed in the United States of America

Library of Congress Cataloging-in-Publication Data

Saint Germain (Spirit)
Beloved Saint Germain's talks / by the ascended master Saint Germain through Godfré Ray King.
p. cm. -- (The Saint Germain series ; v. 13)
ISBN 1-878891-56-1
1. I AM Religious Activity. I. King, Godfré Ray, 1878-1939. II. Title. III. Series.

BP605.I18 G463 1993
299' .93--dc20

93-6193
CIP

DEDICATION

WE dedicate this Book in loving Gratitude to our Beloved Ascended Master Saint Germain for making it possible for us to have His Gift of this Ascended Master Instruction and the Knowledge of our own "Beloved Mighty I AM Presence," as given to us in this "I AM" Religious Activity for the Spiritual Advancement and Enlightenment of mankind.

We thank and bless Him for these early Talks that contain the Wisdom of the Ages, which He gave through Beloved Mr. Ballard (Godfré Ray King) in the presence of Beloved Mrs. Ballard and son Donald, their staff and guests. We are Eternally Grateful for His Explanations of how the Great Law of Life acts for the sincere Seeker of the Light, and how each spoken word, properly applied through Conscious Command, becomes a Magnet of Light drawing us upward and onward into "THE LIGHT OF GOD THAT NEVER FAILS"!

Forever in the Service of Beloved Saint Germain,
"I AM"
SAINT GERMAIN FOUNDATION
SAINT GERMAIN PRESS

TRIBUTE

BELOVED ASCENDED MASTER SAINT GERMAIN, we thank You for this Magnificent Instruction You have given us in this thirteenth volume of the Saint Germain Series. We are eternally grateful for Your Wisdom, Your Dedication to all Life, and Your Goal of Eternal Freedom for all mankind, our beloved nation, and the entire world. May we now apply this Instruction in these Talks to assist us to become Ascended Beings, serving in that Great Octave of Light with You and all the Beloved Ascended Masters and Cosmic Beings.

Beloved Ascended Master Saint Germain, we bow before Your Great Light, and we ask You to stand our Guard. Bless, protect, and enfold us in Your Invincible Armor of Violet Flame that becomes our Day Star, guiding and governing our every thought and deed, until the moment of our Final Victory of the Ascension!

"I AM"— THE GREAT COSMIC WORD

"I AM" is God's Name—the Great Cosmic Word!
The Mightiest Sound that man ever heard!
The Great Cosmic Power fulfilling each Call!
The One Mighty Self that rules over all!

"I AM" is God's Light—now clearing our way!
Enfolding us here and holding full sway!
Releasing all Gifts from Life's Mighty Heart,
And holding us close—ne'er more shall we part!

"I AM" is God's Love, now blessing each one!
Healing forever with Rays from the Sun!
Transcendent It flows—in, through, around, above,
And in us abides—the "Presence" to prove!

"I AM" is God's Power—now carrying us through!
Light opening our Way—and raising us too!
We give It to all, and stand unafraid!
Perfecting all things, and never dismayed!

"I AM" is God's Might—the Great Freeing Power,
Compelling release from discord each hour!
And raising us all to Light's Cosmic Realm,
For by that Great Light, all else we o'erwhelm!

"I AM" is God's Peace—all Life's Mighty Goal!
Light's Great Divine Plan—all Glory untold!
All Victory comes through from God's Glorious Hand!
The Great Cosmic Word is now in command!

Chanera

CONTENTS

BELOVED SAINT GERMAIN'S TALKS

By The Ascended Master Saint Germain

CHAPTER I

January 4, 1938

LOS ANGELES, CALIFORNIA

Beloved Ones, if I can assist you with your questions, I will be very glad to.

Question: You know the 100% Group was allowed to be brought forth so the Students could adjust themselves so You could appear in Your Tangible Bodies. What would You do with those who are not one hundred percent?

Saint Germain: Blessed One, I would not change the situation at the present time at all. We shall endeavor to release a Force there that will either make them give obedience or withdraw. You see, many of them got the idea that if they would sneak in there, they might see one of the Ascended Beings. Knowing that that was the great intense desire of many, consequently many came in with no thought of purification or giving obedience, and were foolish enough to think that We would not see that.

But let Me say this: there is not anybody who can prevent Us coming forward when We choose to do so. Now, those who have practiced deceit—not anyone else—they alone will pay the penalty, of course, because they all knew better. This is the one reason why it was magnificent when the Outline was given. It was simply an opportunity for them to be reminded of the obedience necessary. When they are not willing to do that, then they place all responsibility upon themselves.

You see, this is a very difficult thing; you cannot say that to them in public. But when those individuals sign their name to an intent to their "Presence"—which that 100% Pledge is—that is a very different thing. Therefore, whatever they lack at this time, that will start into action and continue to expand until one day they give the obedience that is necessary.

From time to time, there is no doubt you will find individuals who should not come in; but remember this—and this, I am sure, will give you great release in that respect. You see, We can do so much more now, since the time has come when the Free Will of the individual may be set aside. We can release Powers of Force, if necessary, to bring a very quick, definite change where conditions are too destructive—which We could not do before without someone in the physical giving Us the opportunity to do it. Of course, in cases of crime or something destructive there never has been any obstruction to that; but I think you will find that several of those people will just naturally drop out now.

Just like a year ago—four or five people came to the Shrine Class with a silly psychic prompting within themselves that they would make their Ascension there. If people are silly enough to do that, what can you do? Just let them alone.

You see, the human beings who think they are going to win the Victory without any effort are mistaken; they just cannot do it. But I want you to feel—to ease your precious Hearts—there is not anything that is going to stop Us when We wish to come forth! I want you to feel that.

Question: Should we go to San Diego?

Saint Germain: Well, it would be a glorious thing; but I think it would be wise for you to remain here and be at your Groups, because you have so little time to do that. And will you take the message to them of My Love, Blessing, and Gratitude; and will they kindly stand loyally together and give these Decrees while you are absent.

Question: Are there any special Instructions you would like to give for the Group Work?

Saint Germain: Only to keep all reminded of the need of the obedience to the "Presence"—that means by harmony in their feeling and earnest, intense Application. There are a few who almost make "over" Application. I mean by that, they keep at it too long. I tell you, I have watched it among the general activity of the Students. *People should give fifteen or twenty minutes of dynamic Application, then go on about their work; and if during the day they want to repeat it, very well. But at least twice or three times a day decree for specific things, give dynamic Application, and then take your mind off of the problem.*

It is so easy in the old so-called meditation, and even in the Application today, if the person is not by nature dynamic and begins to give Application—if you could be present to notice, you would find almost from the first Application, just a gradual letdown in the strength with which they come forth in the Application. That is the thing to be avoided, because you had better give four or five dynamic Decrees and stop, than to give seven and begin to wane on the last two.

If you want to shatter a boulder, you drill a hole, put in the dynamite, and explode it. That is power and force. When it comes to the outer activity of humanity, generated viciousness needs it—*requires* force, and your dynamic Decrees. That is why Beloved Lotus had such tremendous results with the vicious forces that were being directed at her—that she recognized in an instant, and flew right back in its face, like an explosion; and It shattered the thing. That went right to its creator because she sent It forth with terrific power.

Question: How is the new Group in Boston doing?

Saint Germain: It was very fortunate that the Emerys stepped in there, in Boston. It was just at a time when very much was needed, and they have established a joy and enthusiasm that was needed there above all places. They have a clean, light, beautiful place now in their Reading Room for their people to meet in, where all the Groups can come and meet under one general focus. Oh, it is a beautiful place. They have done the redecorating in beautiful colors; and all outside is light, wonderful light, overlooking the park. It is a place that is right and deserving.

I say to all of you, watch out that you do not let anyone make any criticism or feeling toward the Messengers, because that would be striking at the Heart Center of Light. Don't have any opinion about anyone. Let all be free to go forth in their work, and give all you are to support them with your love, kindness, and blessing. I am watching very carefully over everything. I am determined to bring about the conditions that I want. It can be done; and I know your Hearts are all so loyal, true, and right, that you are willing to make the human do anything that is necessary in order to come to that point.

I want to take you people to the Cave of Symbols and the Royal Teton in your physical bodies; and if you will give Me the obedience that I have asked for, you will have it. I cannot tell you how soon, and do not plan on any specific time; don't let the human begin to set its own plans, but just leave it to the Wisdom of the "Presence."

I say to you though, Dear Ones—I know I have said it before, but still some do not comprehend. Dear Ones, *even if it is only five minutes, start in and make definite Application morning and evening, no matter what the pull of the outer things are.* Now if you will do that, then the conditions will all be so much easier. It is up to you to determine what you are going to do with the time before you, but this is the thing: if you will give your morning and evening Application—it only takes ten or fifteen minutes—then you will establish conditions about you for the things that arise, for the energy, the Directing Intelligence for the day; and things will just move with so much greater speed that you will find you have an hour or two hours more.

Don't think I am saying this unkindly, for you know I would not; but if you were to see sometimes how the mind sort of wanders and is not quick and alert, you would be astonished. If you will watch yourself, you will notice every time, that follows some little feeling of irritation or discord, or a sort of confusion comes into the mind that does not let it act as quickly and alertly.

Here is the thing I am going to suggest to you tonight, which I have not before. A half hour before you go to make your Application—probably you would not have that much time in the morning; but in the evening, a half hour before your Application, say: "*'Beloved Mighty I AM Presence,' give me the Ascended Master Contemplation!*" Then as you enter into your Application for whatever it is, you will find a firmness and alertness and a quickness in the feeling that you release, which will be surprising. Everyone watch this, and see when you go to do your work, watch your Application, and see whether you feel it is not kind of "blah." If you do, don't make one Application until you release that out of your being. Get yourself into that enthusiasm, and then let loose, because it does so much more. You do as much in five minutes as you cannot do in fifteen minutes if that "blah" feeling is there.

I never saw such a magnificent Manifestation of that as the other night in the great Class. I want to tell you, the way the Power in those individuals rose and let loose was unparalleled by anything I have ever witnessed; and it shows every person can do it, for this was a wholly unprepared thing. It was exactly like when the "Presence" released the Power through Beloved Godfre's body to assist David Lloyd. Don't you see, it was an unpremeditated thing. It released right there the same, identical Manifestation. I tell you, had We chosen to utilize that energy for a Manifestation there, We could have shown that audience one of the most magnificent Manifestations any Group ever saw; but the energy was needed for the Protection of America and gained the Victory in the percentage that was to be gained—so We could not use it.

That is the power of concentrated action and force, because that was actually force released. Now there are only two Groups here that have been doing that. They have been getting that into one Focus. That is the reason tremendous Work has been done in your Group, and is the reason I would like to have not one thing occur that would disrupt the present conditions.

There had been gathering vicious vortices of forces over America from Boston and Seattle; but when the tremendous Decree went forth on the evening of the ninth day of the Shrine Class, It shattered every one of those vicious vortices that had been established. I want the blessed Students of America to know what a mighty, concentrated force of action does.

You all seem to be in this room during the time we are conversing, don't you? From the appearance standpoint, that is true; and yet, you have been definitely with Me around My Table in My own Audience Chamber in the Cave of Symbols. Well, it is a very comfortable place, I assure you. I am very happy in that Audience Chamber, because it was My own Creation a long time ago, and the walls were My own Precipitated Substance. They are beautiful. It might sound foolish to you, and you might think that I am still a searcher for antiques—even the Messenger does not know yet: that magnificent table in the Audience Chamber in the Cave of Symbols came from the Andes Mountains in South America. Would you think it possible that that could be transported from South America to the Rockies and placed within a room in the heart of a mountain? Can a mechanical genius figure that out?

Question: If you can transport the pictures and the other records, why not these?

Saint Germain: This is quite a different kind of thing, a substance—but it does not make any difference. The Law works the same.

Since Bob, Rex, Nada, and Pearl are returning to India, I can say a few things I would like to. I have the greatest encouragement watching those blessed Children. You never saw anything like it. Their enthusiasm seems to grow each day. Naturally, because of that great happiness and joy in what They wish to do, of course it makes it tremendously powerful; and when They start to do something, They find the Power They are releasing is just beyond words.

You will understand, Dear Ones, what a tremendous thing it is to be lifted out of a world of limitations and enter into that Freedom which They are experiencing now. It is so recent that They still maintain the enthusiasm—not that They lack in poise in any way; but the enthusiasm is so very wonderful, it just makes your Heart leap with joy to watch Them operate. Sometimes, at a distance, I watch it when They do not know it, and it is beyond words.

Question: Would the Great Law permit—as we call It forth in the Name of the "I AM" and the people of America, and to You and the Great Cosmic Beings—the sudden dissolving of those four vortices of the activities, like the communistic thing?

Saint Germain: Yes, make the Call which does give

Us the Authority and Power to begin action on those activities and the individuals there. You see, up to this time We could not interfere with them; but since that puts them within the scope where their Free Will can be set aside, I do not hesitate to act.

Question: Wouldn't the sudden dissolving of that substance shake them up plenty?

Saint Germain: Oh yes.

Question: Are there any focuses in Los Angeles?

Saint Germain: Yes, there is one here; but the principal part of that is focused along the coast where it is easier of access, because they have been very cautious. That is the reason they use San Francisco and Seattle, and much of the distribution has gone through individuals carrying it to other points. If the officials had known what some of these individuals travelling were carrying, they would never have seen daylight again.

Question: What kind of Work do we do out at night?

Saint Germain: Marvelous action in the projection of the Light Rays, the use of the Sword of Blue Flame. That is the reason why, wherever it is possible, get to bed by twelve o'clock. I do not mean that you should feel tremendous strain. It does not make any difference whether you are together or where you are, you will always go out in this regular Work.

Question: Can we go out if we are not asleep, if we make the Call?

Saint Germain: It is much better to have the body asleep, because for certain Work We need to do things in the outer world. We must have the connection with the sleeping body to give the energy for the physical things. Why do the blessed ones just fly from one extreme to the other? You know, those blessed individuals who have so much time, if they would get the needed rest and make their dynamic Decrees, they could do perfectly wonderful things.

This Activity has been marvelous because there has been no attempt to force membership. That is why you cannot go out on the highways and byways and drag people in, because if you do, you will pull in a lot of people who are just curious—and in that, have conditions to handle that are wholly unnecessary. You see, that is why advertising could not be used in this Work. Oh, if you had, with all your strength I doubt if you could have survived. I doubt it very much, because once you begin to advertise a thing that is so in opposition to the previous understanding of people, you have no idea what comes at you.

Now this is getting momentum enough, where there are enough of the Students issuing these Decrees and present in all the Classes, that it overbalances much of that. But imagine today, going into a wholly new Class of five thousand people who know nothing about this—why, it would take a giant to stand against it!

Question: I felt You were letting it grow strong slowly.

Saint Germain: It had to be. Oh, We would not dare let too many new people in even yet, only according to the strength of the Students and Group Leaders. For instance, you could take a Class of one-third Students and two-thirds new people and handle it. The Students have come to know that their part in that Class is to hold a certain protection for you, and they naturally do it.

You probably think I am very human this afternoon, but I want you to feel My nearness. *I don't hesitate to use your own language to make you feel My nearness;* but you remember that wondrous, wondrous statement: "Two people standing side by side—one may be taken and the other left." That is the great Law of Selective Discrimination which is operating in the Great Cosmic Light. So, there is no question about those who should be protected;

and there is no question about those who should not be protected. Even if they run away from It, they would be sure to be in Its Radiation.

Therefore, one's attention upon the "Presence" is the only safety there is in such conditions. But this will be a vastly different thing than any cataclysmic activity that has ever occurred—very, very different, because for the first time that great Selective Intelligence with the Cosmic Light will be acting within the Earth.

So, I hope by your return from the East in July that this whole thing that We started out to accomplish will have been accomplished; and when It is, It will be the greatest Accomplishment, the greatest Victory that anybody has ever witnessed on this Earth. Then will you all rejoice beyond your fondest imagination to know that you were a part of It. I wish I could help each one to feel how definite, how tremendous is this great Invincible Light about you—the most *real thing* in the world—and that all these outer things are the unreal.

I shall have the Joy of My Experience when you begin to see each other out in your Work while the body sleeps—I mean, when you retain the memory of it. You see each other well enough; but I mean, to retain the memory of it. Many people do not want to come back here; but as you become adjusted to it, and because it is necessary, you don't mind it so much. But the Beauty, Power, and Perfection which each one is while out in the Higher Mental Body is so beyond any of this in the outer world, oh, you could not possibly make a comparison.

The Light is the only thing that will handle and govern a vortex of human viciousness generated, because that viciousness is force; and unless something blasts it, well, it will probably continue. That is the reason why so many people oppose the Light, for those people who still have vicious things in them don't want to hear that, because it scares them. I tell you, it is a good idea to scare some of them.

When that and the Entity Decree came out, they realized that you meant business and that this was no society evening; and I tell you, they began to realize it was more than for just a good time. Dear Ones, you may think it is rather stern; but to be without something to do, without something to keep the mind occupied, is one of the most dangerous things in the world because it leaves you an open prey for all things to drive into the mind.

Question: Could we know something about the last third of our human creation?

Saint Germain: What would be your judgment? Wouldn't you think that each individual should take care of one-third, at least? You know, that is a great deal—to have two-thirds of your own human creation taken care of. However, you know the Great Law does many wonderful things. Well, Dear Ones, do you not see how easy and quick it would be; just as quick as one maintains self-control and harmony in the feelings, it would be so easily and quickly accomplished.

Question: Would it not be well to use the Statement: *"There is nothing hidden that is not revealed"?*

Saint Germain: I tell you, Dear People, if you would do that earnestly and tenaciously twice a day—release It dynamically like an explosion of feeling—you would be amazed what would be revealed.

The human is such an unstable creature. It will take hold of a thing and be very enthusiastic every day, then pretty soon it forgets. I do not mean one could keep up a long line of Decrees—you could not do it; it would take all day. But after all, there are certain things—now I am speaking of your individual use; and if it needs correcting, let Me correct the idea now. It was never intended that all these Decrees be given all at once, every day; but they are given because certain ones create certain feeling—and they can do with four or five Decrees what a hundred could not do otherwise.

You know, you ought to take yourselves in hand and bring yourselves into line. When you have a certain amount of sleep, get up and go about your work, and really feel a responsibility to your life, your world. Don't feel that the world should carry you around on a golden platter. Just enter into that joy and enthusiasm of service. You can have a real good time now, so just buckle in, take hold, and enter into that. Go into it with a vim and vigor, and mean business. Just feel the happiness of joy and enthusiasm of your work.

You children must not think Me unkind because I say these things—because something has to awaken you to that feeling of something to hold your attention on, more than just yourselves. You see, where the human has had its own way for a long time, it objects like thunder to give way; but I tell you frankly, unless it is brought into obedience, it won't release the Glories of the Light that are within you. It won't do it. But there is such power, such positiveness in you if you just take control of the human and make it come into obedience. It is the same with any human being. It has to be done if you are going to win the Victory which your Heart craves in the Light.

Oh, it does not make any difference, Dear Ones, even if you had ten million dollars; it is not a matter of money conditions. It is a matter of the release of your own physical energy and keeping the attention of the mind upon the constructive things. That is the requirement in this outer world of activity today. You see, a few people—and I can see so many—have gotten the idea that because I made the Statement, because I had brought one into physical perfection without having done any physical exercise, that does not mean that every human being can do that at the present. But the need is to keep the mind from running around and dwelling upon things that it should not dwell on, because the human mind unoccupied, I tell you, will soon do it; and I have never seen anybody that can prevent it. That is why employment, service of some kind that utilizes a certain amount of physical energy, is a marvelous thing for most people.

Like the individual many years ago in Ohio who was ill in bed and had been for months; and it was pouring rain, and this Great "Presence," seeing the need of a neighbor, said to this invalid, "Get up, go and render this service." She could not believe her ears, at first. Again the Voice repeated the words to her, and again she did not respond. The third time the Voice spoke to her, she got up out of that invalid bed, and went out in the pouring rain in her nightgown and robe to the neighbor's and rendered that service, and was instantly well. This is what obedience means.

Question: Do I have to do physical work, or can I hire others? I don't mind doing those things, but I don't like to do them; and I feel there are so many people who can do it.

Saint Germain: It is not just a matter of housework, but it is a matter of fixing your attention and the releasing of your energy upon something that keeps you really occupied. We want you to feel no undue responsibility; but you must feel that you are the constructive power acting, you see.

The principal reason I am speaking of this is because of the element that has been brought into your homes several times, and has opened you to the conditions that followed. I say to you tonight, Blessed Children, do not listen to any silly stories that come to you; do not enter in nor take part in that. Simply say: "We will call the 'Presence' into action; and further than that, we will have nothing to do with it." Keep yourselves out of any gossip and don't be drawn into it, and you will find marvelous blessings. You accept more in your feelings than you have any idea. Perhaps days later you find you have, and that is why I am trying to guard you to absolutely refuse to be drawn in or listen to it. Nobody, I don't care who it is, should enter into this energy. I am not criticizing you, but I see the conditions. I see the things that you need so much to bring you up into that Perfect Glory you can have. You can become a Perfect, Blazing Glory.

Be sweet and kind; but if necessary, be firm. But be sweet and kind everywhere you move, and especially among the Students; and do not let them hear you say one thing off-color or anything that could be construed as being crude. Don't let any expression go forth that is crude, because you are looked upon as the example to the people of the world. Everybody is amazed at the Power you could have. People are amazed at the Power you have in the Decrees and the work you do. That is proof of the Glory that is waiting to come forth in you as you do that and keep yourselves free from all kinds of gossip or being drawn into those things. Do not take part in it. If someone comes to you and wants to suggest something, say, "Call your 'Presence' into action, because outwardly I would not know anything about it." Insist upon it, and do not let anybody get you to pass an opinion on what anything should be. Then you keep yourself free from any vortex of discord. I feel now, if you will take that firm stand as I have suggested, it will be a tremendous help in dissolving completely this whole vortex of viciousness which has been generated here.

I am sure that that last day of Class was the most wonderful thing. The love that those people poured forth, the way they flew to America's defense, was the most wonderful thing ever witnessed in this world; and the way it awakened the love to each other was the most beautiful thing anybody ever witnessed. That is the reason I am prompting you in these things, so that you can release the utmost possible of the Light within you—because it can be very wonderful.

Well now, there is no use talking anymore. We shall have to discontinue sooner or later. Beloved Ones, know My Love and that of the Ascended Masters enfolds you always with the fullness of Its Protection, Blessing, Directing Power; and We try to amplify your Call for the release from the Treasure-house to abundantly supply everything that is required.

Know how grateful I am for all the blessed Service rendered by each one in the Class here. I am proud of you, very proud of you. To be able to stand up and serve with a smile on your face, in the face of that vicious vortex, was something which in itself was a miracle. So, just rejoice that you have the strength and power to do it; and know that each day brings that in an increasing, intensified activity that is without limit.

With deepest Love and Gratitude I thank each one for all of your blessed Service. Good night.

CHAPTER II

January 27, 1938

SAN FRANCISCO, CALIFORNIA

Beloved Messengers and Staff, it is a very great Joy to see how well the response has been since the Radiation in West Palm Beach. It gives Me very great Joy and great Encouragement that that which I have so much planned upon is possible.

I am going to say something to you tonight that I have never said, which I think will give you great happiness. While at present I may not mention them, but if you realized the powerful friends you have in physical embodiment in America—and some of them are never very far away—your joy would know no bounds.

Let us rejoice as never before. Oh, you Blessed Ones and the Blessed Students of America, oh, that you could realize what a Tremendous Service has been rendered in these three years—inconceivable to anyone but the Ascended Masters, because unless you saw from the cause and effect standpoint, you could not possibly comprehend.

I would suggest to all, that you give less and less

attention to any destructive gossip or reports unless you are able to verify them and find that they are true; and when you get reports from different parts of the country that this or that is so, I would not give it a moment's consideration unless you are able to verify it.

I am quite longing for the day when your vibratory action is to the point where I can bring forth certain truths concerning the physical octave, because if once you understand that, everything in this octave would take on a different color; it would change. May I say just this much. Almost everything in the human octave is man-made laws and conditions. It has been so diverted and distorted from the original Divine Plan, that you would hardly recognize it unless you saw back into the Divine Pattern.

Mrs. G. W. Ballard: Is that why I have felt such a terrible emptiness in the music in the past few years?

Saint Germain: Yes, and that is why so much of the tomtom and broken element in the music has come forth, because the more confused mankind become, the more that thing drives in to shatter the vibratory action of the finer senses. I would suggest to all of you, if you are in a place where the jazz music is part of it, charge and draw your Tube of

Light powerfully about you to shut out that vibratory action from your feeling world. You are at a point where any one of you can do that, if you will.

The Great Tenor and the Goddess of Liberty are present with Me tonight for the Work They wish to do with each one of you, so make yourselves lovingly receptive to that Radiation which They wish to give you.

I suggest now that each one of you be as careful as possible—I know the many provocations—from allowing yourselves to voice any kind of criticism or "opinion," shall we call it. I am sure with most of you it is not criticism; but it is often expressing an opinion which would seem like a criticism concerning persons, places, and conditions. Your need today is to hold yourselves as tranquil and harmonious as possible.

You see, Beloved Ones, won't you understand with Me, when you see all the magnificent things that have really been accomplished under the conditions that have existed, then think what a magnificent thing it would be if there were, every moment of the waking and sleeping state, a perfect feeling of harmony, love, kindness, and cooperation from each one of you to each other and to, shall we say, persons, places, conditions, and things, even though they might not seem deserving of it—yet for your own sake, to reverse from your own contemplation that which has discordant conditions. That is the thing in a nutshell. But especially among yourselves, *don't let one feeling of unkindness or an opinion go out concerning each other.*

Tonight I feel more encouraged than ever, that such a thing can be established; and when it has been held for a sufficient length of time, you will see wonders in your midst that you never dreamed were possible—as soon as that has been maintained long enough, because in this now everything is loving, kindly cooperation. If somebody does something that does not seem to be correct, don't have any opinion about it. Just call the "Presence" into action to produce Perfection there, and then shut your own feeling off from acting concerning that particular incident or whatever it may be.

Everyone knows definitely the need of this, and knows how futile it is to pass opinions, because that is the thing that is preventing your achievement. Oh, any feeling of discord or irritation will prevent it. It is not so important to outside things, although that should be avoided; but the important thing is to avoid that on the part of each other in the Student Body. Don't let anything of any description irritate or disturb your feeling toward each other; for that is where I want to bring to a certain condition the natural laws of your own lives, and begin to produce those so-called miracles in your experience. Of course you all know there are no miracles—*miracles are God's Way, uninterfered with by mankind*—but We use that expression as a means of producing that which is unusual to the average experience. I feel so surely that you will be able to do this. Oh, if you only knew what it means, there would not be anything in the world that would create disturbance within you.

This Class will be so wonderful! Be just perfectly calm and poised. If any fanatics should come in and try to create any disturbance, just be calm and serene until they are out; and then go on with the Work.

Within these ten days I have been able to do in Washington that which I would have thought was incredible five weeks ago. So, We have much to be rejoiced about. Oh, Blessed Ones, feel and know with such earnestness and power that all appearance in the government less than Perfection has no power. All appearances less than Perfection in aerial service activity have no power, and the same in industries. When you send out your next letter, will you put a line or two in and say that it is My Wish that all assert more and more firmly that all human appearances less than Perfection have no power, because it does mean so much. That going forth in the mental and feeling world of mankind gives the people—even those who do not know anything about this—a firmer conviction and assurance that these things, although sometimes they seem drastic in appearance and dangerous, yet they have no power. If, in the outer world, enough of humanity would withdraw that power and say to those forces with intense feeling that *they have no power,* you would have miracles!

I tell you, Dear Ones, even with all that you have felt, you have no idea what tremendous accomplishment has been in your Thursday-night Classes when you draw such enthusiasm over your calling forth one-thousand-dollar bills into your hands and use. I tell you, it is a magnificent thing going forth in the mental and feeling world. Remember, *what your attention is upon, you become! What your attention is on, you bring into your Life Stream for activity and use!* It is magnificent! And why? Because everything that is generated in a tremendous spirit of joy and happiness goes forth with a power of accomplishment inconceivable without it.

Now, that is why in all Application, with the exception of certain vicious forces, this powerful and tremendous feeling is a desirable thing to use for the average thing, even toward some vicious conditions. If one could release that great enthusiasm and joy in knowing they have no power, that they are dissolved and consumed, it would be an astonishing thing; but when things seem serious or dangerous, it is not always easy to generate that great joy and enthusiasm. I do congratulate you on your ability to call that forth from that marvelous group of people.

How patient one must be with the human. The way individuals twist things that they hear is a caution, but it just means keeping up your patience until finally they begin to hear straighter and straighter. The Messenger has called their attention to it many times; but Dear Ones, if you could see in the audience when people allow their attention to be drawn by someone getting up in the room and going out, or some little movement that draws their attention—then they miss the whole sentence, or two or three sentences. That is how those distortions creep in. I presume if their life depended upon it, if somebody got up in the room they would not look. Dear Ones, I tell you, the pull of the old habit is a tremendous thing. Many of the Students today are those who have had training and discipline, but they have not brought much of it forth yet—I mean the memory of it.

Precious Lotus, I am beginning to see daylight

for you. I am determined that these things are going to get cleared away now so that you have a breathing spell.

Mrs. Ballard: Please give me some of Your All-Powerful Concentration. That will help.

Saint Germain: I shall endeavor to do so. Shall I tell you that since the writing of this radio activity presented tonight, the Discourse, I find I am able to give you much greater Assistance?

Mrs. Ballard: I felt You so strongly tonight and during the transcribing—more than I have for some days.

Saint Germain: I have accomplished all I can for the present for certain conditions in Europe, and I shall be hovering very closely in this Class. So when you have time or make effort at any of the Work, I shall endeavor to give you such calm Concentration and Assistance that It will make it very rapid and easy for that which you wish to do.

Mrs. Ballard: Shall we get those three Outlines ready first, before we get the Magazine out?

Saint Germain: I think I would, before the next Book; but I would go ahead and get the next Magazine ready as fast as you can, so as to try—Charles Sindelar, bless his Heart, really, he is deserving now of as much as possible—to get the material to him on time. He has been willing to work night and day, so I think now I would try and set other things aside and get that Magazine copy out to him as early as possible. Then as soon as you can, get those three Outlines ready.

The human is a very curious thing. If it is expecting something, it is like it hangs up in the air until the thing is in their hands. They would not settle down and go on as long as they are expecting something, whereas if they would settle down, they might get it sooner.

I smile to Myself so many times when the various individuals are decreeing to Me and decreeing for the Messengers to be there, when they know already that they are booked; still, they keep on decreeing for them to appear at a certain time. Well, bless their Hearts, while they are doing that, at least they are out of mischief; at least it keeps them out of the outer world!

Mrs. Ballard: I was never as grateful in my whole existence as I am that You have given us this Law, that there is something to shut out that outer discord.

Saint Germain: Precious Ones, if this had not come forth today, your Beloved America would have been in chaos I do not care to attempt to describe—and yet, the insanity of those vicious creatures is so steeped that they cannot see it.

Why, when human beings sought evidence of a Supreme Presence and Power, in the Name of God if the experiences of the Class Work and the Dictations are not sufficient, I don't know how it would be possible to give you more. When here, before thousands of people, these Dictations were given, then to try to assert that this Information in the Books was taken from other books—what are they going to do about the Dictations here, the very same marvelous information given. If that was taken from books, well, what about this? Don't you see the insanity of the foolish human creatures that can't see beyond the end of their nose. Talk about discrepancies! Are they not having more discrepancies than anybody else?

You Blessed, Precious Ones, I hope tonight as never before in your lives you can feel how fortunate you are. Oh, Beloved Ones, that you can feel the fullness of it. If you only knew it, you are set apart from the rest of the world—a privilege unparalleled in the history of the Earth, even in the past in the Retreats, because here you have an opportunity to win the Victory in most of the conditions of the outer world, which is the greatest Victory of all.

Mrs. Ballard: I hope someday we can repay You for the Light which You have brought.

Saint Germain: Oh, Beloved Ones, the only pay that I ever want is your Victory! That will be the greatest Treasure to Me in all of the world. Oh, can't you feel, Beloved Ones, how great is My Love for you? I would do anything in My Power to help you win the Victory quickly. You must feel how dear you are to Me.

Oh, the great Rejoicing of the Higher Mental Body of each one of you—oh, Dear Ones, if you could see that. Sometimes that Rejoicing is so extremely great. Remember, your Higher Mental Body has known all through the centuries, and waited and waited and waited; and now when It sees that closeness of the Victory, oh, what a wonderful thing.

I say to you, all of you, please do not be discouraged if sometimes some little thing intrudes for a few hours; but you will always find now that if you begin to reach out and ask the "Presence" to show you the source of that disturbance, you will always be able to locate it quickly and dismiss it. I would suggest this: that at any time anyone finds something disturbing, they just *stop everything for a few moments. Sit down in your chair and be quiet.* Be still enough, and ask the "Presence" to make you feel and know the source of it; then you can easily stop it.

You will find as you keep calling the "Presence" to make and hold that Tube of Light Invincible about you, that you are bound to get where there is nothing that can penetrate that or reach you, no matter what the viciousness directed, because you can make that Tube of Light Invincible. If things arise to be handled, just handle them in that calm, majestic manner. Don't revolve them in your conversation any more than you have to. Take your mind absolutely off those things, and you will find it so much easier to hold the Victory and the Invincibility of the Tube of Light about you.

I wonder if you realize, every one of you, that you are in a position to do everything that Chandu the Magician did—if you could only make yourselves realize it. I cannot quite do it tonight, but I hope in our next visit I shall be able to give you one point of action that will do tremendous things for you. However, I will say this much tonight:

You will remember that your Higher Mental Body knows all about the Perfection and knows all about your requirements here. You have known that the Messengers have been instructed to charge their Higher Mental Bodies to render the Service to the Calls for healing and assistance. You saw the letter, I think some of you did today, where the blessed one called to the Higher Mental

Body of the Messenger and received Instantaneous, Dynamic Response. Now then, suppose you were to call to your Higher Mental Body to do certain things, might it not be interesting to accomplish certain things of your Heart's Desire? My temptation is very strong. I wanted so much to give this which I am intimating to you in West Palm Beach, but the Law would not permit it yet. Anyhow, you can think this over. When you begin to find that you can do certain things with very great ease, don't get excited about it. Take it with a very calm, majestic serenity.

Just be so happy that your whole being glows with that happiness. Beloved Lotus, I am sure—I feel so sure—that you won't have any more battles in the feeling world; but watch My Prompting I have given tonight. If something starts to intrude and you are not able to throw it out immediately, sit down a few moments and get quiet, and seek out the source so you can annihilate that human feeling right then!

I ask you all, think for a moment—why is it that when you don't know the source of a thing, that many times your Application does not reach it? Now will you answer Me that?

Mrs. Ballard: Confusion in our own feelings?

Saint Germain: Well, that is almost it.

Mrs. Ballard: Your attention is on the wrong thing. With the attention on the "Presence" and quiet in the feelings, you would automatically know.

Saint Germain: Yes, but the word that covers the principal activity—you don't know that outwardly perhaps, but it is the lack of *assurance* in your feeling. When you know definitely the source of a thing, the feeling releases. But you see, when you are not quite sure of a thing, there is not the full release of the dynamic power that comes with your assurance in knowing the source of a thing. There is not the force, because when a thing is direct it requires force. That is why dynamic Application released is a force of Self-luminous, Intelligent Substance that annihilates it right then. That is the reason why you can stop a thing instantly, because as a rule the minute you find the source of a thing, you have finished it right then because your whole power is directed upon the objective or that which is generating it. You see the simplicity and the majesty of these things? It is just marvelous.

CHAPTER III

February 6, 1938

San Francisco, California

I congratulate you all on the wonderful success of this Class. We have not time tonight, but the first time we have a little extra time, I want to go into some of the details that took place. I tell you, Beloved Ones, had you seen from the Inner Standpoint even half of what took place in this Class, you would be launched forever in the Victory of your Light. Things were dissolved and consumed that have been active in this city and environment for thirty centuries.

Just be reminded that when the Radiance can be brought to a point where the number of new people who came into this Class became immediately harmonious—to the degree that there was no discordant radiation going forth—that should be proof to every one of you of the Victory of the Light in the Group that has been drawn together, providing you give obedience.

Dear Ones, watch out that your human sympathy does not run away with you under any circumstance. Let each one feel that your Service to the Light is *first.* I congratulate you. I know every feeling that was in your Heart tonight. Let us go on and on into greater and greater Victory in this great Service to the Light.

You see, if you can get vicious forces vicious enough so that they bite themselves, then you are soon finished with them; and I think we are arriving at that point. You know, there isn't anything so amusing in all the world as to see a vicious force thwarted, and they see that all of their effort amounts to nothing. It is really from the human standpoint an interesting thing. However, that is not where We focus our attention, but on the Great Light that produces Perfection.

Now, this is where I am going to have to use the paddle. Every one of you must do more work on your Application. I think it is the outer pull of the seeming need that is keeping the rest of you children from the full Application. So, will you just buckle on your Armor and get busy with definite work. Do not let the pull of the outer world hold you from making your definite Application.

Blessed Ones, I am watching the opportunity to enable all of you to bring back the Work you are doing through the Higher Mental Body, since I asked you to retire and get the body out of the way so the Inner Work could go on. I tell you, the day you bring back that memory, you will rejoice. You haven't any idea, Blessed Ones, the tremendous Work you do from the Higher Mental Body every night your body sleeps soundly. Believe Me, it is no idle thing. I think it is not wise to go into it just yet. You see, I try your patience so severely—not unnecessarily though.

Whenever there is a real desire within an individual to win the Victory, then We want to give all the Assistance We can; but everyone must prove they are stabilized, when they have been so fluctuating through life. Everyone who has a temperament, after giving way to destructive conditions, must prove themselves in order for them to have the realization and the strength it requires to hold self-control.

In the tremendous Service rendered here, this city has been blessed as no other city where the Messengers have been. It just shows what could be done everywhere if the people but realized that their love, harmony, and cooperation make a condition that makes all things possible—that as long as you love, bless, and do not see each other's faults, why, you will find great achievement. Children, you know when they get playing, sometimes have peculiar feelings and actions; so you are not children at play now, but at work with a Joy of Eternal Perfection which is that Service.

Don't you think I am frightfully severe? Does My paddle hurt so severely? But it is nice to have My children around Me before they scatter in all directions and then come together again.

Now I must be considerate and remember that you all have things to do before tomorrow, so remember that My Love and Blessings enfold you. If My paddle was not too strong, you will still love Me, I think, and go on your way happy and rejoicing, knowing your Victory of the Light and of the Classes. As you go forth, do your Work twice a day for the Perfection, the filling of every seat in the Kansas City and New York auditoriums. Charge ahead that Mighty Power that reaches out or enables the "Presence" and the Ascended Masters to reach out, prepare the way, and fill those places.

The radio and transcriptions are doing a Work that is very marvelous; and I say to you blessed ones, do not bother with discordant conditions or individuals. If it is a discordant condition of health, that is quite different; but if it is some feeling of discordant viciousness and condemnation, tear it up and forget it. Someday, by your silence, they will know that something was wrong. Do not waste time and energy on those things.

There is too much of the greatest good that can be done.

Question: As You may have noticed in our Contemplation Groups, instead of calling for things to be done, we have been saying: "*In the Name of the 'Beloved Mighty I AM Presence,' we say to all human creation: NO! By the Victory of the Sacred Fire, you have no power! Your day is done! Be thou dissolved and consumed from the face of the Earth forever!*"

Saint Germain: Stipulate, "*You have no power!*" to human creation and human forces. It is absolutely *imperative* to be maintained. And when you ask that they be dissolved and consumed, I think it is a very important part of the Work; for not only is that accomplishment being temporarily done, but when the Great Cosmic Light in this greater Power descends of Its own Volition—which It will—that means the Activity of that Light will then take over the charge of the quality of mankind and enable It to do in a great sweep, as it were, the dissolving and consuming effect for the conditions that are in the atmosphere of Earth, which it is the province of the Great Cosmic Light to dissolve. That is why in Washington's Vision It was shown—and Beloved Arcturus mentioned It, because They all know that one day there must descend into the Earth this Great Cosmic Light. We cannot always tell just how It is going to manifest. At first It may begin with Great Rays of Light that hundreds of people will see, and they will feel the Activity of the Forces of Light. Should It decide to act in that manner, you would see the greatest transformation in human beings you ever witnessed in your life—oh, I mean that ever was witnessed on Earth!

Only when the Light takes on sufficient Manifestation and the people begin to see from the human standpoint the Victory of the Light, will they begin to come into line, as it were, and realize that this which has been mentioned for many, many centuries—well, in fact, ever since the seventy-thousand-year-period civilization—in each age this Idea has come forth. Of course, you are only cognizant today of your own present time.

Dear People, today the Truth carries with It *Application,* and the Understanding that mankind must make Application to release themselves from the conditions for which they are alone responsible. How in the world would they go on for the next million years—if the Law of Life and Light permitted that—in the same condition? It is only this marvelous Understanding that is bound to bring the freedom of mankind, and make mankind alert to the things that they have just ignored completely.

You can say a thing is needful; but mankind, in the density into which they have drawn themselves today, unless some Application is given them, they are like children—helpless. That is why the old occult laws had to be set aside—they were doing far more harm than good, expecting mankind to reach out in the mental and feeling world and gain the Understanding of these Great Laws when the density was so great.

You see, the density has become so great that they cannot comprehend anything else until their attention is drawn to it. Then feebly they begin to think and become just a little more alert. If you saw in many of the Classes—and of course it was more noticeable in this Class; but in almost every Class that has been, if you saw the change from the beginning, the first day and the closing day, you would absolutely—unless you saw it with your own eyes—you would certainly say it was incredible. The change in the comprehension, the change in the alertness! When that is pounded at them with dynamic force—which has been necessary—then they begin while they are in the Radiance, to awaken, be alert, and feel more; and ofttimes for a considerable period afterwards they retain that alertness which was practically unknown to them before.

Now in this Class—you take the Students who have been in most of the Classes—a tremendous Work was done.

Mrs. Ballard: May I ask You why I awakened the other morning with that thing—a mailed fist? Was that a black magician?

Saint Germain: Yes.

Mrs. Ballard: Was he from Europe?

Saint Germain: He was the black magician who was the driving power back of so much.

Mrs. Ballard: I felt that, when I made the Call to take him.

Saint Germain: You know, it is strange; mankind has seen that, even in the newspapers—that black, mailed hand. It has been in your newspapers, showing that somebody sensed close enough to draw that much of it forth. Think of it, you today who are responsible for so many of these black magicians being seized and bound, this one was the one who caused your death in Egypt. That is why you (*Lotus*) handled him and brought it back into the physical, which enabled his physical body to be destroyed.

Mrs. Ballard: I mean the one here the other morning.

Saint Germain: Both of these.

Mrs. Ballard: Did I bring this fellow back too?

Saint Germain: Yes.

Mrs. Ballard: Tell me, did I do something with the Blue Ray from my own "Presence" to help dissolve him?

Saint Germain: Yes. You dissolved the image which he projected, which made it possible for that physical body to be dissolved.

Mrs. Ballard: He was in physical embodiment?

Saint Germain: Oh yes, both of them were. The one in Los Angeles was the one who caused you to be burned at the stake as Joan of Arc. This one was the one who caused your death in Egypt; so retribution does come, does it not?

Mrs. Ballard: I was not afraid of either one, but this thing the other morning was a definite action; or was it because I happened to see it?

Saint Germain: Yes, there was a somewhat definite action. They won a temporary victory, but all to their end. *Therefore, there is no force of darkness that can ever win the victory.* Never! They seem to have temporary results, but often it is an open door to their complete annihilation. Won't you feel that, toward all destructive forces toward yourself or this Work? They really have no power! When you have come to know this now with dynamic Application and know the Power of your "Presence" at the same time, then do you not see the tremendous

Power you carry when you use that Decree?

Now I must say good-night; otherwise, we will be going along here until the wee hours in the morning. It is not right and just, and I should know better; so I will say good-night to you. My Love and Blessings enfold you all to your Victory; and remember, the important thing is not to get on each other's nerves.

Question: Any special instructions for the Thursday night 100% Group?

Saint Germain: I think they are very marvelous. I would suggest, as Victory did tonight, that you hold them all firmly to those three Decrees, because it is very vitally important at this time for the Work in hand.

Question: Will You tell me wherein I have fallen down in my Application?

Saint Germain: The feeling in your mental Application is abundant, but the feeling is not always following the Application. If your feeling always followed your intense Application, you would perform miracles, because your feeling is intense; but you have not been aware in your earnestness of your outer Application, that the feeling was not always following it. So if you will watch that, you will find it does not run around "Robin Hood's barn" when you want it to be concentrated.

Question: How long should we use the Violet Consuming Flame?

Saint Germain: I think if you use it intensely, five minutes, three times a day, that is quite sufficient. That will keep dissolved anything that is there. There is so little of your human creation left in any of you. I think it will not be so very bothersome.

Question: Did I do the right thing the way I talked to that woman this morning?

Saint Germain: There are many of those individuals who are more or less psychic. When you begin to do physical things for them, they will hang onto you like a barnacle; but watch out in the future, all of you, and be very careful about that. There is always a reason people get into the conditions they do, so don't be over-sympathetic. The Light within her was strong enough to draw her to this Light, and if she will apply It she will have her Freedom; but she must not think you are going to make the Application and assist her physically all the time.

I would suggest that in the future when you render a service, which you have done so wonderfully to so many, cut them off right there. Don't let them feel they can follow up and begin to cling to you. It is very important because there are many people who, seeing your great loving kindness, will work every means to keep following up, leaning on you to make Application for them and give them material assistance. So whenever you give help, not only issue your Decrees silently that they stand on their own feet, but if they physically try to lean on you, simply shut it right off and say: "You must not do that. You must stay in your own environment and depend on your own Application." It is very important, because you cannot carry people to Heaven on your back; and there are a few who think there is a possible chance they might ride there, possibly unobserved. So, you cannot let them do that.

Question: Does everybody have to be present at the Class to have their human creation dissolved?

Saint Germain: No, there were others outside. Now I am really closing. Good night!

CHAPTER IV

February 8, 1938

Los Angeles, California

Beloved Ones, this is indeed a rare treat. I want you to know, Beloved Children, that you are gaining a Victory with a power and speed that will delight you. To every disturbing suggestion say, *"You shall not enter our world and its activity."* You can say that to a person, place, or condition. You can say that and have Victory right away. You have had the experience to show you how necessary it is to know the source of anything. It is sometimes imperative to reach out in consciousness and find the cause of a thing. When you find that such a thing comes from you, you can concentrate your full force upon it and dispel it. Call your "Presence" to show you the source; then you can call the Higher Mental Body to dispel it.

As you draw your Armor of Light, It grows more and more Invincible each day. When you harden metal, you heat it to a certain degree, then dash it into water, then watch the heat recede until the metal gains a certain hardness. When you call forth your Armor of Light, you charge the energy into It and It becomes more and more Invincible. When your Armor of Light reaches a certain point of Invincibility, It then holds Its own to a certain degree. If you discontinue, you would notice in a week the letdown.

You can become sensitive with power. You can have a great calm, but be sensitive so you can detect things in a moment. You always come into a powerful sensitiveness in your Governing Power.

If a thing disturbs you, get still first. Call the "Presence" to show you its cause and what to do about it. Call your "Presence" to reveal to you whatever you ask to be revealed. When you call a thing forth, the attention is held steady; and every time you add to it at each Call, you add power to it.

If the Student will train himself or herself to realize that at each Call he releases Light-Substance, he will feel that Light—Self-luminous, Intelligent Substance—pour out at each Call. It knows no resistance nor interference, and keeps pouring into the objective at each Call. Remind yourself: "This Call is Light; and each time I call, I add to it more Self-luminous, Intelligent Substance."

On Venus they have machines for taking dictation and making it into a book immediately. It comes first in a picture with all details shown. In the Light are held all pictures of all things that are. The picture is the Light and as soon as the attention fixes upon it, out of that Light comes the understanding of how to produce it.

If the human would not get irritated or impatient, the whole thing would be revealed easily. These things are all the Activity of Light. It is all a matter of getting the feeling into the susceptibility of the action. When confusion or uncertainty enters the feeling, it scatters the force which you would otherwise concentrate upon your objective to produce the results you desire.

In regard to money supply, oh, it does not matter how much you require, just say: "*'Beloved Mighty I AM Presence!' Take up this Call, and bring this house, money, or airplane into our hands with plenty for its upkeep!*" Leave all to the Wisdom of the "Presence."

Up to this time mankind has done everything the hard way because they have so long forgotten the "Presence."

I have watched the effect of occultism for one hundred years, and I have not seen anyone who has had any results. The occult student begins to *imagine* results, till they do not *accomplish* anything at all.

The work of invention of the future will be done by clean, clear, fresh minds who are not confused by technicalities. What is to come forth We have now in the Retreats in mechanical form, and it can be reproduced easily. The mechanics of the coming age, which are to transcend effects of the Earth's gravity, must be of a rate of vibratory action more rapid than that which is within the Earth's currents. They will therefore be unaffected by those Earth currents.

As the Cosmic Light comes forth into more and more Dominion, you will find, as these conditions are brought forth, they will be regulated so the completed action will come forth quickly.

The need of today is to get away from all that produces friction. With the new power mechanism, airplanes within the air currents can anchor in midair and yet hold up twice their weight. A magnet holds things to it by currents of energy. You can project a Ray that is a current of energy which is a thousand times greater and more powerful than any magnet. When regulated, and the currents within your mechanism are greater than that of the atmosphere, you are unaffected by it.

Gas engines will cease to be. All power units of

the future will be things that call forth currents of energy. Then, things that call forth currents of energy will have more power than a diesel engine.

You have no idea the stubbornness of human intellects. You must bring such individuals step by step, until they step right out into Perfection, because they have been steeped for centuries in their limitations.

We have a metal today in Our Retreat that the bullet from an elephant rifle will not even dent. It is one-fourth inch thick. It is bulletproof because it has a resiliency that does not let things affect it. If an airplane made of it was hit by a shell, its radiation would not permit the shell to explode.

All these planes will be pointed front and back, so passage through the air will have no resistance. They do not know yet how to regulate the bevel. At higher altitude the sharp nose is required.

All the mechanics must come forth from the Octave of Light or Venus. They are already thought out. The modern mind does not conceive, by itself; it only accepts what has already been conceived.

People of today are not creators, for they do not draw forth Ideas from the Great Central Sun. The Ascended Masters draw these things forth from Their original Astronomical Center, the Great Central Sun of our System.

As you begin to rise into a limitless vibratory action, you become that action and thus rise out of all limitations.

The cartoonists have touched upon some remarkably real things.

The possibility of the future, according to the Intensity of the Great Cosmic Light as It comes forth for Its Victory on the Earth, will depend on the condition of mankind in the future.

The Earth was self-luminous originally, and would have remained so if mankind had not imposed discord upon it. Mankind's feeling is a vibratory action; and when individuals have built upon that for centuries, you can realize what vicious destruction comes forth.

Be perfectly still a few moments. Say something like this: "*'Beloved Mighty I AM Presence,' Great Host of Ascended Masters! Make me masterfully sensitive to all I need to understand and know; and see I comprehend all You present to me!*" Then you would know things as easily as you read a book.

Precipitation: In the thought of a thing is the mental picture which forms the cup or mold. The feeling pours the substance into that and produces the form.

Say: "*'Mighty I AM Presence,' You do this!*" Then you use your attention to hold the focus after your

Call. Then all the energy the Higher Mental Body has called forth is concentrated to bring it forth.

The feeling of the unnaturalness of a thing is the barrier that often keeps the manifestation from activity.

From now on, say to everything less than Perfection: *"Oh no, nothing but the Perfection of my 'Presence' enters my world! Now get out!"*

When people bring you gossip, say: "If this thing is true, we shall help them. If it is not, then you are committing an injustice; so let us all go to our 'Presence.'"

The feeling world is one! The mental world is one!

Thank you.

CHAPTER V

February 17, 1938

Kansas City, Kansas

Beloved Ones, We are enjoying your joy! I wonder if you quite understand what it means to release such joy and happiness? It makes almost anything possible of achievement.

Question: Why are not all of our Decrees fulfilled?

Saint Germain: I am eternally grateful that the Queen of Light called the attention of the people to the fulfilling of, shall we say, present and latent desires. Every one of you can look into your life and see where, one by one, present or latent desires have been fulfilled by the dozen. Since you have touched this Stream of Light, how many, many things have been fulfilled? It would be well to check sometimes on yourself, upon the desires that you have had, and see how many have been fulfilled, because mankind is so prone to accept the thing to which they are accustomed, as a natural consequence. Not that it is really surprising, but when you begin to check, see how many things have been fulfilled, both small and great—I mean from your human standpoint.

Question: Are radio transcriptions important?

Saint Germain: If Students will only utilize the material they have, everyone will have the Freedom. But this to Me is the most important thing: utilize all the material possible on hand, but devote the needed time to the magnificent radio transcriptions that I will try to assist you to bring forth. That today is far, far more important than running larger amounts of the magazines.

You have no idea how the attention of listeners on the radio is drawn to the Books. It is really remarkable; and by that and the fundamental Instruction given over the radio, it enables them to read the Books with a certain amount of understanding they would not have without it—I mean awakening a certain comprehension.

Question: Should we impress the Students with all that is being accomplished?

Saint Germain: Yes. The greatest Power of Light ever known since the Second Golden Age is being released into the Earth at the Call of this great number of Students, and that is the greatest need.

The Students should be reminded daily that this which they are calling forth from the "Presence" is

Light, which knows no resistance nor interference. Once the Students get that idea, they will "mow down" everything in front of them that is destructive.

Question: Please explain about Energy, Substance, and Intelligence You have mentioned.

Saint Germain: I tell you, this is vital, because it is true that Energy, Substance, and Intelligence which goes forth from the "Presence" is Light! It is Light-Substance! Therefore, it is the same as when you turn on the light in the room—the Light dissolves human qualities and discord. If these Students who are having inharmony in their homes, good Heavens, if they would only realize that, they could stop all arguments and would be able to release such peace and power in the home that everybody would become harmonized.

I say to you tonight, *as you value your future progress, do not allow a single thought of criticism, judgment, or condemnation to enter your feelings.* Now I tell you, you are doing marvelously well; but there is still some chance for improvement. It is vital, Beloved Ones! You must realize that you are the Heart of this Great Light that is to save America and the world. If you cannot harmonize yourselves and keep it so, how do you expect the rest of the world to do it?

Question: Please explain the need for obedience.

Saint Germain: I say to you with all the Love in My Heart—and I congratulate you on the Victory you have won thus far; keep it up absolutely, until the full Commanding Power of the "Presence" is in action through your mind and body. *But please do give obedience to the things I ask if you want Me to give you the Assistance.* The human cannot possibly know —it never knows what is best. It gets impatient and rushes in to do the thing humanly that the Powers of the "Presence" would do possibly better. So that is the need: you must all stand guard over yourselves; and as you all know, there is no letting down. There is no failing to stand guard over yourself and your world until your Ascension. What gains momentum? *Your sincere Application!*

Question: What is the best way to proceed?

Saint Germain: With the Power of Divine Love. Once understood, you can cause It to become the Threefold Flame. Do not discuss this with others! We are soon going to bring the comprehension to the point where We can, in connection with the Violet Consuming Flame from below, bring forth the Power of the Unfed Flame from Above, that will make a powerful Consuming Activity; and it is through this Action that We have been able to accomplish all that has been done. We released the Power of the Threefold Flame to meet the Violet Consuming Flame, which makes an All-powerful Activity.

Question: They meet at the Heart, don't they?

Saint Germain: Yes. Perhaps We should designate the meeting point is at the throat rather than at the Heart, because the Action of the Unfed Flame, acting within the Heart, begins to rise from the Heart; and I would rather you think of it as a "meeting." Think of it in that manner—as the Power Center, which is the throat. That will be a tremendous thing to govern and control the power of speech, or shall we say the *impulse* of speech.

Question: You mentioned that most of our human creation has been consumed. What is our next step?

Saint Germain: I would stand very carefully the guard over your feelings for the next few months, until all of the old feeling that is in the atomic structure of the old momentum is gone. It is not easy to explain to you.

You see, in the Light Pattern of your body, the Points of Light in the cells have been clothed by you with discord; and even when the human creation is dissolved—it does not mean that. Let Me find a word that will convey to you just what I want you to understand by it. Let us use "quality." I think that is about the nearest thing We can use. You see, the *quality of the charge* of the "clothing" of the

Light within the cells is the thing that must be purified, after the pressure of the human creation is off. If the charge has been somewhat dynamic, that means it may require some time for that to be released—the *quality* to be released from within the "garment" of that Point of Light, which is the "clothing" about it.

Of course you do not see it, but every Point of Light within your body stands out separately. If you saw it from the Inner state, you would see distinctly the force field around each Light, just as you do the force field in the study of electricity.

Question: Is that in the feeling body—a habit in the atomic consciousness?

Saint Germain: Yes, it is a charge from the habit of the atomic consciousness. That habit has to be stopped. Really, the habit in this instance is what We term as momentum, because *habit is what causes momentum;* and the human atomic structure—it is simply astonishing how quickly it will begin to accept a situation. Oh, about two, and not over three repetitions will cause the atomic structure to begin to accept that suggestion or action.

But I must prompt you again, Blessed Ones! Before you sleep at night and when you awaken in the morning, first stand on your feet. Don't move to do a thing until you *charge your mind, body, and feeling world with the Perfection of the "Presence," with Its Mighty Directing Intelligence, and with Its Enfolding Presence of Divine Love and Infinite, All-powerful Protection.* You would be so amazed if you would just do it methodically. I do not mean by that, do it with just the head. Watch, and do not do it until you have your feeling following your attention and requirement. If you will just watch out that your feeling is following that, if you will train your feeling the moment your attention goes to that, it will surge into action! That is where you get such tremendous blessing and effect—from the *conscious charging* of your mind, body, and feeling world; and if you will do it all the time, you will see the most amazing effects upon your body and worlds!

In addition: "*'Mighty I AM Presence,' charge Your Mighty Power of Divine Love and Harmony into my feeling world and out into my activity before me.*" If you will do this, you will be astonished. Do this with great earnest sincerity and enthusiasm. You see, these things sound so simple; but Heavens, how powerful they are.

I urge you, Blessed Ones, for you are doing a thousand times, or shall I say *giving* a thousand times the Blessing to mankind of anything that has ever been on this Earth since the time of Beloved Jesus. More than that, you are reaching so many more people. I tell you, the Glory of that is worth everything in the world. *Do not allow the pull of things to prevent you doing these things We ask*—a few simple things that will keep you protected and on guard and supplied with energy. It is marvelous!

Question: But some do not have time for Application.

Saint Germain: Do not give them any chance, any more than possible, to hook up some excuses for their not having Answers to their Application. They don't see how that very thing is the most Infinite Proof and Power of the Action of the "Presence"—their Application. The human has to be humored like an infant until it can gain a certain momentum. You perhaps have seen some of it yourselves; for some great strong men and women act just like babies on certain things. They are powerfully strong on certain things, and on other things they are just like babies. Some wonderfully physically strong men act like infants when they have the slightest pain. They succumb to it; and you may observe that when some kind of epidemic starts to spread, it is almost without exception the strong, husky people who get it first—almost without exception.

Question: Because all that energy becomes qualified?

Saint Germain: Exactly. Where the human can get mankind to accept a suggestion, that throws tragic fear into them.

Oh, My Dear Ones, since I have come into the Ascended State and am able to see clearly all the forces that were acting upon Myself and that act upon mankind, I tell you, if you ever want to annihilate the destructive forces, it is then. You have no idea the battle that I had in those earlier days.

Question: Beloved Serapis Bey evidently did too?

Saint Germain: Oh, yes. Twice I took jail sentences to protect ones I loved.

Question: In your last embodiment?

Saint Germain: Yes—one in the embodiment in which I made the Ascension, and one in the previous one. I really, in My last three hundred years, almost four hundred years, I did not re-embody. I just simply changed bodies.

Do you realize, My Dear Ones, what it means when I so earnestly ask you to do these few simple things—for instance, charge your body night and morning. Why, if you only realized what you can do. You can compel your body to take on Perfect Youth, not only in appearance, but in activity. Now, for instance, I might add this thing: *Charge your body. Charge the Currents of Energy into every organ of your body to do its perfect work: your kidneys, your liver, your stomach, your lungs—all the organs of your body. Charge them into Perfect Action.* It is really very vital to charge those organs with that Mighty Energy, causing perfect action in those parts. Why, with you today there is not any reason why you cannot compel every organ of your body to obey you and do its perfect work, because you have now come into sufficient control of your food so that it would be easily done. It would not be easily done if you were cramming your stomach all of the time; but as it is, you are all realizing that it does not require anything like the food you once thought you needed.

Shall I tell you something that is positively the funniest thing in human beings? You know how you all used to eat, twenty or thirty years ago? Do you know that the energy required to handle all of that food was ten times that which you required for your own action.

Question: Isn't that awful!

Saint Germain: Absolutely. The consuming activity required within the stomach was ten times the energy you used in your daily action. So it is not any wonder that the stomach sends back what you send down sometimes. I do not know what mankind would have done if it had not been for that. But think of all the civilizations—when they came to this point where Perfection had to come in, or complete the destruction of the outer form, in every case (and We have records of it), in every civilization that went down through cataclysm, they gorged themselves and could not handle the food. Just think! In every civilization before its annihilation, that has occurred—just an orgy of gluttony. Really, if this Work had only done one thing, it would have rendered an inestimable Service to mankind—because this Teaching, through the Power of Radiation, is *absolutely compelling from within,* the refusal of acceptance of so much stuff in the stomach.

Well, if you could see, oh, My Beloved Ones, just for one hour, what certain quantities and kinds of food, and I mean by that, what *starches* would do in your system in twenty-four hours. For instance, just as an illustration: when you used to eat spaghetti, macaroni, fried potatoes, and about five or six slices of bread; and I mean by that, you know the sandwiches you used to eat—double slices of bread with just a tiny little bit of substance between; and sometimes if you were very hungry, you ate four or five. If you could see for twenty-four hours the struggle of the stomach to eliminate and throw that out of the system, I tell you, it would be the greatest revelation ever given to mankind!

I would suggest to Beloved Godfre that he does not mix grilled pineapple and cauliflower.

Mr. G. W. Ballard: (laughter) Was that what was the matter with me? That certainly had a battle down there, all right. It is still growling. I appreciate knowing the certain combinations that certainly don't set well internally with me.

Saint Germain: Precious Ones, it really is so easy if one just looks at this from a natural standpoint. How wonderfully you can govern these things that make the struggle of the human seem so much less.

Question: What can we do to release tension?

Saint Germain: Since this comes to My Attention, I am going to suggest if all of you will remember where Chananda asked the Children to stretch out on their backs without any pillow and relax every muscle of the body. If everyone would practice that for ten minutes, you would be surprised how it will relax the body. In almost everything you do you are sitting more or less like this *(slouching)*—sitting at the desk, typing, or whatever you are doing. Even when you are standing, you more or less slouch. Those habits form; and if you will watch yourself and practice this, you will have immediate relief. That is the inclination—to slouch—especially when you are a little tired. Immediately when you do that, you cramp the whole nervous flow of the spine, and that is how people get under such tension.

Question: How do we keep from accepting human suggestions?

Saint Germain: That is the way you gain Mastery and Victory. We give it no power to act, refuse acceptance of it, and call for its annihilation. That is the way to dispose of those things completely. Just because a thing seems to have gone into action in the outer is no reason to accept it as a permanent thing. If you did that, you would give way to all human creation. That is how We never accept a thing that does not express the Perfection We want. Even though the human sense of it may have gone into action, still do We not accept it, because if We did We would give it the power that would sustain it indefinitely, and We cannot afford to do that.

Especially in the physical octave, We bring forth such tremendous Power and refuse acceptance of all things less than Perfection; and if you will do that, you will one day have only Perfection acting in your world because you are constantly charging It forth. Do you realize that when you call forth a Charge for some definite Perfection, that you are holding a large percentage of that Charge in your own feeling world, because it is the Law. Whatever passes through your feeling world, you must retain a certain amount of it because it is the Law of Life. And that is really the compensation for the earnest Desire for Perfection, and the reason why I have, from the beginning, ever since the Beloved Messengers went forth, kept prompting them to keep prompting the people to keep *charging themselves;* for if your feeling is following the attention, you, in a short time, would get so you could release on instant demand any amount of energy—Directing Intelligence of what you require—right on the dot at once. But you see, unless you realize that all practice gains momentum in that, you are very apt to feel as though you are using unnecessary time.

Oh, My Blessed Ones, my goodness, ten minutes of Application in a quiet state will sustain and do more for you than hours would in the state when you had allowed disturbance to get in during that time. That is why, the first thing on getting on your feet in the morning, *make the Charge and compel the feeling to follow the attention.* You will soon gain a Power of Control and Momentum that everything will be right there on demand. There will be no question about it at all.

Mrs. Ballard: You have no idea unless you have

experienced it, what some little seeming interruptions or interference does when I am working. It breaks the current, and sometimes I don't get back in it for hours. During the writing of the radio transcriptions, I was interrupted so often I wonder that they came out at all.

Saint Germain: Under those conditions, We had to govern that for you. I tell you, it is unparalleled in the history of the Earth what has been done in the writing, the editing of the Books and all the material—and how, in all the things that have driven in up to that time, you step through those curtains to the audience. It is an unparalleled thing in the history of the Earth, I want to tell you; and I congratulate you both with My deepest Love and Gratitude—"I AM" Eternally Grateful. It only proves what can be done when there is sufficient determination.

Mrs. Ballard: Shall we rush to get out more Books?

Saint Germain: No. Why, if these people, or if the whole world for that matter, never had another Word—if another Word never went forth, there is a thousand times more material than is required to give them their Ascension, because the reason for the Application is there.

Question: Is it all right to continue to wear furs?

Saint Germain: I think it will not be long until there will come forth material that will amply replace that. You see, in the understanding you have today, there is not anything which you cannot govern and regulate by moving your hands over the coat or skin and throwing off that substance, dissolving and consuming all the influence of the animal which was absorbed. You can make it free from that.

Mrs. Ballard: May I ask, in the calling forth of the Light-Substance, when we say to the Great Ones, "Replace it by the Cosmic Light-Substance," does that come from a different Light-Substance than the Ascended Masters' Octave of Life? Does It come from the Great Central Sun of our System, or does that come from the Temples of Light in the Ascended Masters' Octave? It seems I have been finding it is more effective when I use the word "*Cosmic* Light-Substance" instead of just "Light-Substance."

Saint Germain: Oh, yes. *Anything that is Cosmic, while It affects individuals and groups of individuals, always has a world Activity.* For instance, when you call on the Cosmic Light, It may produce the results you want in individuals or groups; but still It goes on in Its Expansion in the world Activity, because it is impossible not to act that way because that is why

It is sent forth.

Here are two illustrations: the description the Messenger gave of the expansion of the Light above the Shrine Temple that spread and forced the sinister activity back out of the borders of America —that was a Cosmic Activity and was the Cosmic Light-Substance. Again tonight when the Light was released in the Reading Room, that same Activity went forth for the city here, in a lesser degree. These Activities are Mighty and Real, and you have all seen the results of that explosion of Light in the Shrine Class. Look at those spies that were following you for months and months. They have disappeared. So you are having the most marvelous evidence before you of the Action of the Light every day.

This is a very definite thing, Precious Ones. Please understand it. This Activity is a wholly different thing than ever on Earth, because this is gaining a definite forward movement and activity that is a permanent thing. Please understand it, because if you do, you will see how every step gained individually or for the Nation is a step forward to that time when the Light will come forth and take command of individuals, and compel the Light within to release and take command of the mind and feeling world of the individual.

Then they can be directed to do the things necessary; then will Divine Justice reign.

I want to tell you, surely you must see that this Activity at the Shrine, when that Great Cosmic Light exploded there and did this tremendous thing—you see the evidence before you. Well, if that would do that, then what would ten-times-that-released do in addition to it? That was a permanent thing gained. Those things do not have to be repeated. Whatever is gained by that particular Release will hold its own, because the Light holds Its own. That Cosmic Light-Substance is here to stay. Absolutely!

If only the blessed Students would believe what I say to them and ask them to do! You will probably remember in the Shrine Class when I first began to give the idea and use of Our Consciousness—why, My Dear Ones, if you realized once what that means! That is the Consciousness that knows the Victory. *That is the Victory of all We have attained.* That is the Feeling of Victory. You see, it is all that is contained in the *feeling of accomplishment.* The intellect—I mean *the thought form of it and the whole achievement is there in the Ascended Masters' Consciousness;* and if one would realize it, you can call that forth into use because We have given permission for it. Why, transformations inconceivable would take place as surely as one did it earnestly; but in all you do, if there is not the full feeling of enthusiasm and earnestness, just wait for a few moments until you gather that. If you are just doing it from the intellect, it is only a small part of the result desired because the intellect is not the thing that does it. It is very splendid—because if you are exhausting yourself from Application, it is from the intellect, and you have gained no particular achievement.

Question: Is this same thing true of prayer?

Saint Germain: Yes. Prayer was even worse, because oh my, my, my, so few prayers were anything but just the lips. Oh, it is only where some great crisis or emergency was, that prayer was put forth with dynamic feeling. Then it was always answered. I venture that ninety-five percent of all prayers were just lip service, because you see, the human when it becomes accustomed to a thing begins to parrot, almost without exception.

You saw the magnificent difference in San Francisco when you stepped up the Decrees and began to get enthusiasm into the energy. To Me that is a magnificent example to all the Students forever who were present, because there was not one in that room that did not feel the relaxation and rest. It is the same thing in the singing. If you let down below a certain tempo, it is like dragging you downhill. The same way with the Decrees; when they reach a certain rapidity of activity, that passes that balance into the dynamic, constructive Work. I would suggest in the future that in your Decrees and singing, if they are not keeping up the tempo enough, stop right there and explain to them they will have to step it up, and you will get results.

Question: I have a question about my Tube of Light. Sometimes when we are in the atmosphere of discordant people, are we supposed to visualize the Tube of Light and expand It way out? Do you want us to expand the Tube of Light to enfold the whole audience when we are leading Classes, or do we just hold It close about us?

Saint Germain: Hold It around yourself only. Never expand your Tube of Light to encompass the audience. When you go to encompass the audience, make them stand on their own feet, and draw your own Tube of Light around you. Otherwise you are opening your Tube of Light around you, and that must never be done. I think you had better take your firm stand and not open the Tube of Light to anything or anybody. If you want to give assistance, then call to your Higher Mental Body or the Light

Ray to give the Assistance; and that keeps you out of their world.

The same way in your meditation: Silently call and visualize this Ray going forth from your Higher Mental Body enfolding the audience; and then you remain physically untouched and you are rendering a Service far greater than if you expanded your Tube of Light, and it does not endanger you by influences coming into your own circle, because the Master never does that. If He expands a Circle of Light about the audience, He holds His own about Him. You can call the "Presence" to do that which is required; but He never lets anyone within His own private Circle; and it would be well for you to take that same firm, determined stand.

Question: Where does the Armor of Light come in?

Saint Germain: That is the clothing, really. You see, your Armor of Light is like a close-fitting garment and comes within your Tube of Light.

Mrs. Ballard: I have noticed whenever I have been sitting there projecting, and when You begin to do certain things and I begin to take the Flame from my Heart and clothe the audience, that is a Force; and It goes there and controls everything for the time being.

Saint Germain: You see, that is quite a different Action. Again, when you call forth the Power of the Unfed Flame or the Threefold Flame to do that, you have a wholly different Action from your Tube of Light, because that is the Higher Power of Action—the Threefold Flame and Unfed Flame.

Mrs. Ballard: Do we go to the Cave of Light in our Etheric Body or Higher Mental Body?

Saint Germain: Which do you suggest?

Mrs. Ballard: Well, our Etheric Body is nearest our physical body; but our Higher Mental Body is perfect and doesn't need any perfecting.

Saint Germain: That is a very good conclusion. I congratulate you.

Mrs. Ballard: Haven't we really been having the Action of the Cave of Light since the time we started?

Saint Germain: Oh yes. I am glad to hear you determine to go in the Etheric Bodies, because that is really where you bring It into the outer more readily.

Mrs. Ballard: What have we been working in?

Saint Germain: The Higher Mental Body. You could not work in your Etheric Body in the Work you have been doing.

If you go to the Cave of Light, you won't need your Sword of Blue Flame. You would be surprised how little about you needs to be cut away—I mean of your own creation. Of course you need the Sword of Blue Flame from outside influence; but because of your individual human creation, you don't need It so much.

We must not prolong this longer, as I must return to Europe for the completion of Work I have been doing for seven months; and bringing It to this point, I trust It will be accomplished before seven o'clock your time here.

Mrs. Ballard: Could we help if we went with You in our Higher Mental Bodies?

Saint Germain: I think I will leave you an Escort to the Cave of Light.

Do you, Dear Blessed Ones, realize what a determination like that means, for I felt the Charge within each one of you when you determined to visit the Cave of Light. Do you realize what a tremendous thing that means? These things are real; and when you determine to go to a certain place like that, you go. Don't you see, with that determination there isn't anything that could stop you but yourself? When you determine to go to a place, you actually go. Now, this being a Decree of your world, you are to determine whether you want to go in your Higher Mental Body or your Etheric Body; but you have already specified the Etheric Body to go into the Cave of Light, and that you will bring a greater Charge into your physical body.

Mrs. Ballard: Let us go tonight to the Cave of Light and ask the Beloved Great Divine Director to consume the last fragment of our human creation; and when we come back into the physical, use all the Powers of our being and the Powers for our use—which "I AM" with Ascended Master full Perfect Balance; and use these Powers only as the Ascended Masters do, and use that in the physical octave.

Saint Germain: Excellent. And with My Love, Blessings, and Gratitude to one and all, I say good-night.

CHAPTER VI

March 10, 1938

Cleveland, Ohio

I bring you Love and Greetings, Beloved Ones of the Light, from the Great Host who are ministering to bring about the great Eternal Victory of the Light.

We are all supposed to be able, to a large degree, to forget personalities; and the Law of each one's Life is going to demand a certain amount of that. Seeing from My unlimited standpoint, I obey the Call of each one's Life through their Higher Mental Body. I cannot be misled by human desires. The individual unascended, can be. Therefore, it is My Privilege to attempt to guide and direct until such time as individuals come to the point in the clearness, in the receptivity of their own "Presence," they do not mistake the direction of the human for the "Presence."

Therefore, I know sometimes blessed ones have thought Lotus was severe in her holding guard over the correction in the requirements; but one day you will find it is not.

Mrs. Ballard: I am grateful that You relieved my mind, for I felt maybe I was wrong.

Saint Germain: My Dear, you are being prompted because of the responsibility and guard that it means. If you two Messengers are not to give obedience and guard this Work, then who is there to guard It? If I cannot have you to give Me obedience, and others to give you obedience, then where does the obedience come from to hold the Work pure and unadulterated?

Mrs. Ballard: May I make a request for everybody, ourselves included, tonight; and if I am intruding on anyone's Free Will, then I withdraw it. "*In the Name of the 'Mighty I AM Presence,' in the name of the American people, in the name of the sanity of mankind, I ask You and the Great Divine Director to take out of every one of us, every fragment of the human—cause, effect, record, and habit, and everything of the human; and blast it, the last fragment, until it can never act again; so each one can serve to the maximum of their own 'Mighty I AM Presence,' that there can be done for America what needs to be done, and ten times more than You hope to do!*" I have said repeatedly for a long time, *please don't let us want anything but just Your Way.* I ask that; and if I am intruding on anyone's Free Will, then I withdraw it from that person; but I do ask it, that You may do that which You and the

Great Divine Director know must be done for the Students and America.

Saint Germain: I have the Right and Authority to ask it; but at the same time, unless We can have the *willing* obedience from each one, there are yet certain things upon which We may not intrude.

It has been Our Hope ever since New York, to be able to dissolve and consume the last vestige of each one's own accumulation of human creation and set aside time and space for each one, that they might more easily hold the obedience and have the dominion to allow this Great Work to be done. We have been very patient, but the time is demanding, and I trust no one will blame Me for this firm, determined stand; but the Life Stream of each one compels Me to demand it, and it must be given regardless of human desires.

Mrs. Ballard: May I say to You—I am speaking now for myself—considering what we have all done in the past, in this embodiment at least, the work we did in the outer world, the things that we thought we were doing that were right, serving life, and the conditions in the outer world, may I say that the hardest work any person ever did in the outer physical life, all of it for all lifetimes we have ever lived, still would not be too much to give and do over again a thousand times for the privilege of being near You and carrying the Light for the Freedom of America and the sanity of mankind. Were I to do it over, I would work a thousand times harder for the privilege of obeying You now.

Saint Germain: Thank you with all My Heart. That is true and real obedience.

Mrs. Ballard: It would not make any difference what this Work demands of us, still it would not be a fragment of what we have given to the outer world and had nothing in return.

Saint Germain: I want to say to each one of you tonight—and your gracious and kindly remarks enable Me to bring it forth—if individuals in the outer understood what full and complete obedience means to the "Presence," to Us who represent the Activity of the "Presence" in Its Perfection, you would know so definitely that everything then of the activity in the outer would have such unsolicited assistance unknown to the outer world, that everything would come into order, Perfect Divine Order with an ease, a speed that would be almost inconceivable to the individual who did not, within their feelings, give that full and willing obedience.

Owing to the conditions—if I seem severe tonight, bear with it, because you do not know the conditions which I know; and unless I can release sufficient Radiation and Power through the Staff, you might meet conditions wherein it won't be so easy to be guarded. I do not want you to fear, but there are still attempts being made to interrupt this Work; but if a sufficient harmony and willing obedience can be given by each one of the Staff, so I can release through the Staff the Power of Radiation—you will not see It, but It will go forth, nevertheless—We can govern these outer conditions so that no physical thing intrudes.

Mrs. Ballard: I have tried since I wrote that article on the Power of Peace I read over the radio, to charge the Staff three times a day with Your Power of Peace.

Saint Germain: That is a very good suggestion. Will each one of the Staff take that up and charge yourselves and each other either with My own Power of Peace, or Beloved Jesus', Nada's, or the Divine Director's, or all together, as far as that is concerned?

This attempt—I cannot go into details and explain to you, because I do not want to get your outer mind on it; but the conditions, until after your trip to Washington, require the most powerful protection and calm Power of Radiation. After that—I do not mean anyone should let down on their protective power—but after that the conditions will be very much more easily governed, but so far We must govern these conditions from the Inner standpoint.

You see, this Work is not just a matter of My walking in. I can go in and get what I want. There is no question about that; but this is the Work of the Students, in preparation for the things which are to follow. There is no use of My going ahead and doing these things without sufficient Application of the Students in the environment who are supposed to be a part of this. I cannot be after them all the time and tell them the demand. If they really refuse acceptance of the human appearance and call the "Presence" into action with a calm, determined, earnest desire, the human will not ride in to make them uncertain of which quality is acting.

If individuals could forget each other for the time being, things would be more easily adjusted. People begin to blame one another and build upon things, until the first thing they know they create a condition which has to be dissolved—because these days, in the increased Power of the Cosmic Light, individuals are releasing energy and power of which they have little concept. Especially when the feeling is charged with a little defiance, or disturbance enters in, much more feeling is released than is even imagined. It seems so strange when We have pled with the people so long, that they will still keep giving power to human appearances in the feelings, when in the intellect they know the actual truth—that they have no power. We just have to keep on trying.

If there is anyone who has anything in their feeling, known or unknown, that feels that I am not Real and Tangible, and that the Messenger has anything to do with these Dictations, then you must get it out of your system, because that cannot remain in your midst. I know absolutely everything that is going on in each one's thought and feeling. I am never deceived with what is in the feeling and motive of the individual; therefore, do not think for a moment that I am. But these things have reached this point now where We are so near reaching the apex.

Oh, I do not mean, Dear Ones, that one has to be as perfect as the Ascended Being for this to be done; but I am only asking certain simple things that anyone can give to make it possible. In Kansas City when this great percentage was attained, and now when we have the opportunity to go on expanding it, surely there is no human desire that could have any part in it.

Oh, those Blessed Ones who have so recently accomplished the Ascension go forth with that great Love, pleading with the people, trying to have them understand that only so recently they were in limited forms, and now are Free. How many there are in America today who could have that Freedom even as quickly, but all desire to have a feeling concerning another must vanish.

Oh, Beloved Ones, *love and bless each other as you have never known or thought possible, and refuse to let one word or a single feeling arise in you of criticism of each other.* It must be done. If you forfeit the right now, then God help you. I do not mean by that that any harm would come to you, but it would mean you would be again in the outer world from which you came. Oh, I wonder if you realize that you are no longer of the outer world. I wondered, oh, so much, and I longed so much to see in the audience (when the Great Divine Director said He held them in that Globe of Light drawn from the Cave of Light in India) those who realized a single thing of what He meant and how real it was. But after all, great and tremendous is the Victory being won, in spite of all.

Steadily and surely is vanishing the so-called opposition to the Light, and the time is very short now until vicious individuals who begin to put forth that viciousness toward the Light will last but a short time. Their ignorance in their viciousness toward the Messengers, toward the Light, makes no difference—the reaction will come.

Not so large a number, but a great and loyal, tremendous love goes up from this place; and there are about two hundred people here from whom the most intense, loyal, wondrous love and gratitude is released to the Messengers and the Great Ones for all that has come forth. Of course, that is equal to two thousand who would be lukewarm.

Will each one of you, as you have the opportunity to talk to people, stress the one point that in all their Decree Work they are releasing into the mental and feeling world of mankind—so far-reaching—these qualities or whatever is called forth, and that there is no limit, really, to it. You see, Beloved Group Leaders, in the future try to understand the need of your holding fast to the Ascended Masters' Words. Look how long the Messengers read from the manuscript. While they have a privilege the Group Leaders do not have, there is not one thing they ever say that is not Our Words from the Dictations that are in the Books or private. The outside world does not understand that perhaps, but nevertheless it is true. Therefore, that accounts for their success in this great achievement. If all the Group Leaders understood the need or reason for using the Ascended Masters' Words that are Cups that carry those Qualities into their Group Activity and their Decrees, they would have no difficulty in making and holding harmony in their Group Activity.

You will notice in every single instance where discord came in, it was through an individual trying to assert their human opinions about it. In every single instance you will find that is the case. The moment a Group Leader or anybody begins to lose that humbleness and feel their authority to dictate to somebody else, then trouble is brewing because the very condition will open them up to the discord that is surging everywhere. But that need not be done. If every Group Leader and Student knew, really knew in their feeling, that their every motive was known to the Ascended Masters, that there was not anything hidden, how different everything would be. It would keep them in that humbleness. It would keep the discord from intruding so often.

I do not think, Beloved Ones, that the Law of your Life Stream will permit Me to give any further promptings. I am not definitely sure of that tonight; but when that Life Stream says, "Stop," then I too must stop. I wish you could know how amazingly infinitely you have been privileged. Never in the history of the Earth has as much prompting been permitted by the Life Stream of individuals as in this case, but it is because your Light must be very great in order to permit it. So won't you accept that, in all the joy of your Heart—that because the expansion of your Light was enough, I invited you to come into the Heart Center and be a part of it.

I want all the Staff to know how very wonderful, and what our Blessed Lotus' courage has meant to each one. Many times she has given the prompting when this Messenger would have been silent. So, know how great your blessing is; and you cannot help but know, each one of you, that only the greatest love and kindness goes out from each one. Never in your life did love pour out to you from any human being as the love pours out from each one of them to each one of you.

Please feel with Me tonight how real all of this is. This is no imaginary thing. You are entering into the Great Power and Mighty Stream of Life. You are dealing with the Mightiest Laws in the Universe in this Heart Center of Light! If It is to govern America, if It is to govern and save and bless mankind, then you must know how Infinite is Its Power. Oh, you only see a fragmentary part of Its Manifestation yet; but won't you be patient until the Law sees fit to show you the magnificent splendor of Its Power, Radiance, and instant Obedience over destructive forces and powers of which you cannot conceive as yet.

You are not dealing with the Messenger's imagination; you are not dealing with some shadowy condition of Life, but the most Real and Powerful Activity—the Power and Force of Light!

Everyone's Life Stream, Students or otherwise, is the thing that decrees what is to be done for them. You might decree a thing outwardly or desire a thing outwardly; but if it was contrary to your Life Stream when you had entered into this Stream of Light, then it would not be answered, unless by that answer it brought to you an experience that would be the lesson to be learned.

We hope for many wonderful things in this Class. So, will everyone enter in with the joy and happiness and enthusiasm that is yet greater than any you have experienced, and just let the flood of your being and world charge forth. Oh, Beloved Ones, if you could look—now this is not human sympathy, but if you could look into the Hearts of mankind and see what is there, how gladly and willingly you would render every service of your being. Unfortunate humanity is crying out as never before in the world for help, for freedom. It is this great mass pressure—and our Blessed Lotus once saw it as great rollers of time that are rolling humanity in between those great rollers, compelling that Life Stream to come into Divine Order.

To some it may seem very painful. To others it will be an extreme joy and gratitude. But if all understood, even the painful letting go of the human would be a joy too exquisite to describe.

Oh, to once stand in that Gateway of Freedom where We stand! Oh, Beloved Ones, can you feel with Me for a few moments what our Blessed David Lloyd, Rex and Nada, Bob and Pearl, and the Rayborns feel—that which They feel in the opportunity to reach the Goal of Eternal Freedom forever! Human desires sink into such insignificance after centuries, and lifetime after lifetime of struggle—the same old struggles again, again, and again with no perceptible change; yet, then to suddenly step into the Stream of Light, the Pathway of Light that is like the movable steps in the department stores, that aside from your own movement is carrying you on and on and on, rapidly into that Eternal Freedom of the Light. Perhaps there would not be any better illustration to you than as you walk up those stairs, as they are moving, your own effort is there; but underneath you is the Power of Light carrying you forward with your own efforts. That is what We represent to you. The Ascended Masters' Power, Consciousness, and Light is just like that moving stairway under you that is carrying you on more powerfully than your own effort could possibly do, and yet taking you to a sure, definite Goal with that obedience to Our Requirement.

Oh, do you not see, Blessed Ones, that in your joyous attention to your "Presence" and the Great Ones, in that great Perfecting Activity taking place within and about you and your feeling world, how the whole world without must come into that glad Divine Order and Perfection and Harmony of all that you require for your happiness, supply, and comfort in the outer world. Do you not see how it would be impossible for you not to have everything in Divine Order in your outer life? Oh, not that individuals might not try to oppose you at times, not at all; but that has no power, it has no effect upon your life so long as you do not accept it. Oh, how individuals who feel unkindly to the Messengers or to the Staff are just pushing themselves farther, farther, and farther beyond the periphery of the Light. What a pity! Is it not true that when anger and viciousness beset the individual, all sense of reason and justice is lost? They see nothing but their own fiendish picture of the human desires.

May I say to you again tonight, that in all My vast experience there is no one thing so difficult to endure as to see one here and there fail on the Pathway of Light. I think that is the most difficult thing that anyone has to experience. You do not see in the human octave that which I mean by those words; for unless you saw from Our Octave of Light, you could not understand nor comprehend just what My Words mean. But to Us it is a tremendous thing. And yet, We must always be serene.

We are soon touching into that great Height of Achievement of the seventy-thousand years ago, and whatever Height of Achievement has been achieved since, will all be combined into one; and then I trust—and it is why I have so earnestly been prompting—each one will leap ahead.

May I say something most encouraging to you, in spite of all that has occurred in the outer? Since the beginning of the Kansas City Class, the Light within each one of you has expanded at least one fourth beyond what It was at that time—a very wonderful thing; a miracle, so-called, in itself.

Do you not understand there is not one thing within your physical body that cannot be done by the directing of the Currents of Energy from the "Presence." The directing of the Activity of the Violet Consuming Flame, or the Blue Ray, or the Consuming Flame, or the Unfed Flame, directed and held to a given point, would remove all imperfection there. Won't you all just try it out? Whether it is on yourself or some other body, try directing the Violet Consuming Flame, just like It was intelligent, because It is if It is directed by the Intelligence of your "Presence"; and see It penetrate and dissolve a growth, or see It put Its lasso of Light around that and operate on it and take it out.

Oh, for the confidence in the Power of Light, that you have in the outer things! Is it not strange, Beloved Ones, how because of habit you have confidence—but of course you do, you remove the *effect* of things; but who of you shall say to Me you remove the *cause* by the surgeons in the outer world? Sometimes that effect does not gather again in this embodiment; but Beloved Ones, unless you have removed the cause and the record, it might recur.

Therefore, Beloved Ones, I wonder—you see, I am wondering tonight too—if any one of you could tell Me how much I love you. Is there anyone brave enough to venture?

Mrs. Ballard: More than our outer can understand.

Saint Germain: Quite true. Oh, maybe I am a severe old chap; but nevertheless, I think you will all survive it.

Mrs. Ballard: I wonder that You have not gotten tired of us long ago, and You would let us take our medicine.

Saint Germain: Well you know, I think, Blessed

Ones, all of you have had all the whipping you need—I am sure more than was really necessary; so let us just, as you say, cut it out in the future.

Question: ________ wants a new suit of clothes, and he says he sees that diamond on his hand.

Saint Germain: Tell Me, what would you do were you to awaken some morning with that physical ring on your finger, and your suit of clothes there ready for you?

Answer: I don't know, but I would be awfully happy. Am I looking in vain for my diamond? I feel I could almost see it sometimes.

Saint Germain: Blessed One, it would be impossible in the Light to look for anything in vain that was the Divine Order for your Life Stream. And really, I have been very peculiar throughout all My Life Stream, for I have loved jewels because of the radiance and power they have conveyed. Oh, if you, each one, only knew what stands so short a distance before you, the joy within your Heart would burst all bounds. I think I hear you say to Me some of these days before long, "Well now, where is all this Perfection You were talking about? Why isn't it manifesting?" Now then, can you tell Me what has been achieved while we have been visiting? Now tighten up your suspenders. Sometimes I am strongly tempted to come forth and take you, one by one, in My Arms in congratulations. This started out seemingly rather severe, but it has ended in a Blaze of Glory.

Mrs. Ballard: Can I do more intense work for the Washington Group to push aside the discord, that we may have these Broadcasts? I think I have left them on their own when I have been busy with other things.

Saint Germain: That is quite all right. Don't feel your responsibility for those places and conditions. Do whatever work you feel impelled to do; but don't accept any responsibility, because it is their work. It is they who must harmonize themselves. You are not supposed to do constant work on them to keep them harmonized.

Mrs. Ballard: No, but it being the heart of the government, I so much want the maximum power to be poured out.

Saint Germain: Don't you worry. When you get there your Class will be all right. I may find the way to have some of them cancel their engagement. However, we will see. Do not let those things bother you. Go right on serenely with the Work; and do keep before you, Beloved Ones, that the human appearances have no power. It must be before you. Don't accept anything ever from the appearance world less than the Perfection, for any cause whatsoever, as having power to obstruct or interfere with the Light, the Class Work, individually or anything else—because that is a tremendous part of the battle, so-called, to just simply know that any appearance that attempts to interfere with your world or the Work has no power instantly. Then go on with your Call and Application, but feel that with dynamic Power. You absolutely stop everything, as it were; then as the Power of the "Presence" flows forth, it dissolves and disappears.

Question: Would it help any if we asked Beloved Astrea to hold a Wall of Light around Washington and bind all black magicians?

Saint Germain: Yes, and may I suggest in addition to that, that you *call Mighty Astrea, the Mighty Divine Director, the Goddess of Liberty, and the Queen of Light to dissolve every human focus of discord that has been drawn within the city of Washington.* That is quite as important as disposing of the entities, because there are vortices of human, destructive activities that have been drawn there—about ten within the city of Washington. Call Beloved Astrea to take care of the entities, and the Great Divine Director or Mighty Victory or any one of Those to dissolve, consume, and explode all human vortices that have been gathered there; then consume them, because sometimes you need to shatter a thing before the consuming activity can act quickly. Do as you would if it were something exploded.

As you visualize—you do not need to know just where they are, but into all those human vortices that are there—see the Blue Lightning go into that, explode it; then use the Violet Consuming Flame and consume it. As you make that mental picture, it will hasten and intensify the activity of your Call to the "Presence" tremendously, because those human vortices there are quite as important, in fact more important now than the entity condition. A lot of the entity condition has been handled there, so that is not as dangerous just now as this other condition.

You could do the same thing for New York, but let Me explain to you what happens in this activity I am suggesting. When you call the Blue Lightning into a thing to explode it—you know, just like the roots of a tree: each one of these focuses or vortices there is like a root; and when that explodes, that goes into that, which means into human beings and their feeling world. At first they will be tremendously confused; but as that settles down, they will begin to see and sense Divine Justice of the thing and their mistake or wrong. So, I feel that activity now is as important, or more important than any one thing that could be done just at this time. I am telling you this today because of your own human creation being dissolved; and as you project that Blue Lightning into that and see it explode, then It carries into the roots of the thing. I would call for the cause, effect, and record to be consumed; but in each case, just make the one quick, dynamic Call. Then take your mind completely off it and let It go forth sustained to do Its Work.

Mrs. Ballard: Can you tell me what it was I brought back the other morning when I saw someone standing in the Unfed Flame untouched? Was that my human watching the Higher Mental Body instruct me, or was I watching someone else?

Saint Germain: For the moment you were watching another's experience, and your great intense desire will bring you into the same activity. This observation was the Etheric Body of the individual, and this may be done—let all of you take notice of this—this may be done with and through the Etheric Body of each one, which will carry the Radiation into the physical, causing tremendous activity and change to take place. Now you are all getting a tremendous tip there. You see, did I not keep My Promise?

How great, how great is your privilege and opportunity! Remember, you have the opportunity, the privilege of entering into the Unfed Flame in the Etheric Body, carrying the Radiation into the physical body which would bring about a very rapid change in the appearance of the physical form, its health and perfection.

Question: Should we visualize the Crystal White Light or the Golden Light?

Saint Germain: I think it would be wise not to offer suggestions. Let the Wisdom of your "Presence" do that, for perhaps no two of you would require the same color, qualification of activity there.

Question: Should we make the Call just before we go to sleep?

Saint Germain: Yes, and please don't have any consideration whether you see any immediate result or bring back the memory. Don't be affected by that, just go right on. Before you go to sleep, make that Call. If you understand what I mean from the Inner standpoint—as soon as you cease to look for results, then how much more quickly will the results come. That sounds like a paradox, but it is true.

Now I must say good-night to you, Beloved Ones. Oh, we could go on and on and on for hours and hours.

Mrs. Ballard: Will you make the ears of the world listen tonight, and speak through my voice on "America's Power"?

Saint Germain: God Himalaya has prepared the Currents already, and they are waiting to carry it forth.

Question: Will that go to India?

Saint Germain: Oh yes. So I will say good-night, and all Love and Blessings to you all. May the fullness of that Infinite Light from your "Presence" anchored within your Heart expand, produce Its Perfection, Perfect Health, Strength, Courage, and Harmony in your feeling world of action, and glorify you with a Serenity and Consciousness of Command and Power that compels obedience to the Law of Divine Order and Justice everywhere you move. In the fullness of Its Infinite Power of Light, good night.

CHAPTER VII

March 26, 1938

Washington, D.C.

Rejoice, Beloved Ones, tonight as never before in your precious lives. We are rejoicing too, for in the conditions that threatened at the beginning of the Cleveland Class, to see they have vanished today is a marvel of the ages. I cannot go into the detail tonight to explain to you all of this, but just enough that you may know that some of the very drastic things threatening even in your government, as well as in your Class Work, have been dissolved completely. I am sure you will find a Power, and people will feel a Power in this Class that will silence the human.

Little does mankind realize, and I hope—you see, I am very hopeful; you may have noticed that. Do you really know what that means when I say to you, "I hope"? Do you know that is a signal to you to help? May I remind you that you have two good Friends in the Ascended State who, before their Ascension, acquired the knowledge of the Elixir of Life? That is no myth, believe it or not.

Do you realize what it means to have very powerful Friends? Do you realize that the Great Divine Director has on His "working clothes"? When I saw Him let loose last night, I tell you, My Joy knew no bounds; for I know Him very well, and when I saw that Power begin to release, I knew that He meant business.

With your continued increasing harmony in your midst, I do congratulate you sincerely for being willing to give the needed obedience, because without it no permanent thing can be gained; but in this obedience it makes so much possible. May I make it a little stronger even tonight in causing you to feel your responsibility to the world? If any one of you creates inharmony, either in yourselves or those under this Radiation, then you would be responsible for the failure of the fullness of accomplishment that would otherwise be here; but since I am sure you are strong enough to know this, rejoice with all your Hearts in your ability to serve in this great capacity.

Oh, it all sounds so simple, doesn't it; but it is in the simplicity and freedom from ostentation that the Great Powers of God flow to bless mankind. This child whom you have this letter from, is only one of thousands who has had experiences that will begin to come forth in the world. Here, there, and from all points will come proof of this Great Law; and some of these vicious hounds will shrink up and hie to the woods for the falsehoods that they have spread, proving to the world that they were but claws of the sinister destructive force, trying to prevent the Light coming to mankind; but they have no power! Oh, for mankind to know this.

Unfortunately humanity, when they could and do have the opportunity, oh, so often cast it aside. For instance, this lady came to the Class and was so delighted. And as soon as she got away, the forces came around her again; then she lost it. But you cannot compel people to do things against their own Free Will—they must be left free to choose. The only thing you can do is make the Call to their "Presence" to cut them free; then the Wisdom of the "Presence" will do what is best for them. It is a very serious thing when mankind have the opportunity to accept the Light and do accept It momentarily, and then allow themselves to be drawn aside. It is a very unhappy condition.

Do you realize, Precious Ones, you are like beings of a Sacred, Charmed Life; and you can become more and more that great Charmed Life in which a word spoken in the Name of the "Presence" will release Its Powers into Action.

Do you realize that it was right in this city where Mrs. Rayborn came forth in Her Tangible Body, and it was right here in this city where I answered the reporters at the door in person? Therefore, as the children say in their play, "You are getting warmer and warmer."

Question: Was it in this hotel that You answered the reporters?

Saint Germain: Are you not getting a little inquisitive? Do feel that Light within as never before in your life experience—that Light within you that holds Its Dominion. Remember, *you are clothed with the Armor of Lightning, with the Sword of Blue Flame in your hands; you are shod with the Diamond-tipped Sandals to fill all your outer demands. You are clothed with the Light of Perfection, with Its Radiance growing more intense. It is the Light of Eternity that is your Eternal Defense.* Please feel that!

Do you think for a moment that any kind of human creation would look in the direction of one clothed with the Lightning, with the Armor of Lightning? What does lightning do? It flashes forth its power with a rhythmic activity, does it not? Therefore, if you are aware that you are clothed with the Armor of Lightning, it means flashing! Flashing is that Mighty Radiance from your being, into which no discordant thing could ever penetrate;

and as you become aware of that, whether waking or sleeping, then as you go forth from the body you would be clothed in your natural Armor, which in your human form you must call forth into action. Then as you go forth in your Armor of Light, you would always be Victorious.

Do you know how very precious you have all become to Us, and how We long for that hour when We can precipitate the table, the service, and the food here for you, and you won't have to run around to cafeterias! Well, what has once been, can be again.

Won't you feel all this tonight. Oh, just feel it so real, so true, that with the sufficient intensity of your feeling, We can bring it forth and not have to wait and wait and wait. I do not mean by that, that you must be anxious about it, or anything of that kind; but just calmly and serenely want it now—and as the old Methodists used to say: "Now is the accepted time. I can, and I will, and I do believe." You know, that is the old orthodox idea that "Jesus died for my sake." He didn't; nor, "He died that all might live." But He *did* leave the Example that all might become like Him.

I hardly dare refer to it further, but the Accomplishment of last night was gigantic and, as our Blessed Lotus says, "stupendous and colossal." I literally mean that. Do you not see how sometimes when we go along serving earnestly with no perceptible change, we are entering into those Gates of Glory that suddenly open wide, and there we see before us the manifested Presence and Activity of that great Achievement? Such was the case last night.

You know the Great Ones are very silent, always holding Their own Counsel unless others are to give assistance; and when the Great Divine Director begins to release that Power, He seems almost terrifying to the outer vision. Then you will know that all forces give obedience, and willingly; for that is the Power of Light!

Is it not very beautiful to become versatile? And each one is becoming more and more versatile. I feel very proud of My Family. Do you begin to see what I have meant, and I say this more particularly to Lotus and Godfré, how all that I have said in the past, how it has all been drawing certain ones together—not only because of their harmony, but because of conditions of the past association that make many things possible.

I have never taken it up much with you in this respect, but I want to touch upon it tonight. Where there has been in the past very harmonious association, it means that accomplishments can be had in the renewing of that harmony which has gathered a momentum through the centuries. That is what is about to be released into your midst now.

I am about coming to the conclusion that it is soon going to be necessary for you to know outwardly something about your more recent associations, because in that will be released the feeling I think We can utilize to very great advantage. So I think; however, we will see. But I think before the Class begins, We will try to devote a whole evening to a discussion of your previous association. I am sure you will see the reason for many things today; and really, this follows down more particularly over the seventy-thousand-year civilization. That, to the human sense, just now seems considerable time. After all, in Eternity a year is but a day.

Mrs. Ballard: It is the same Life Stream.

Saint Germain: Exactly. Now that is an idea. Had you thought of it? Isn't that proof how and why there is no time and space? All is just an activity of the one Life Stream. For instance, one of your lives up to the present moment is but an activity, isn't it? In the human clothing you cognize time and space; but after all, when you cognize the Stream of Life up to this moment, you would hardly think of it as time and space, but an activity of your own Life Stream. Just think about that.

I am expecting some of the most beautiful things to come forth in your musical activity. You might not be aware of it, but I am somewhat of a musician Myself. However, Lotus, I am sure that your poetic genius will far transcend Mine; but at the time, I felt quite elated about it.

Question: You do not mean Shakespeare, do you?

Saint Germain: I might refer to that.

Remember, Beloved Ones, when your thought and feeling ascends, your Light expands with great rapidity; but when your thought and feeling descends into human conditions, then your Light shuts off. That is why in every moment in which the mind is not occupied, if it would continue its Call for Light, more Light! Light! Light! more Light!—how wonderful it would be.

Do you realize—I do not feel that you quite do—what that simple word "momentum" means? Oh, My Dear Ones, realize that the continuous Call, repetition of a thing, gains a power of momentum that finally becomes a great avalanche that mows down everything before it. If it be constructive, then all destructive forces are mowed down before it; if it be a destructive momentum, then it means sooner or later the body is swept under by it.

Therefore, there is not one of you so busy that you cannot, many, many, many times during the day in the moment's lull of activity, call for Light! Light! Light! "*'Mighty I AM Presence!' More Light! Blaze forth Your Light through every cell of my body!*"

Before we close I want to draw forth this: *Mighty Power of the Cosmic Light! Come forth in this city! Take Thy Dominion, produce Thy Perfection in the preparation for the Class Work, in the Class Work, in the Presidential chair, in all official places in this city, in all governmental activities. Mighty Power of Light! Take Your Dominion now! Clothe each individual in the Power of Light that compels Divine Justice, which glorifies Thyself, "Mighty I AM Presence," through the Higher Mental Body in Thy Perfect Action, Thy Dominion of the Light!*

Charge into this city Thy Mighty Perfecting Activity of Light in Its Limitless, Eternal Activity! Charge It forth sustained! Mighty Astrea, send Thy Legions of Blue Lightning to seize and bind every entity in this city. Take them into the Octave of Light, and take out every spiritualistic medium in this city—every entity. Send It forth now, and take them away from those mediums. Hold such a Circle of Blue Flame around them, that no longer can they come near. Take command of ________; put such a Circle of Blue Flame around him that his whole human creation is dissolved, and that he awakens into the Light; and all these mediums that have gathered here, make them powerless to act any further. Make them feel the Power of their own "Presence" until they turn their attention to It and know that It is Real, and all desire for spirits disappears from their feeling world, and they are cut free now, this hour!

Charge forth and glorify this city as the City of Blazing Light! Great Powers of Light, draw Thy Mighty Power of the Unfed Flame, and if necessary make It Visible here, that all the world may bow before It and give obedience.

Take command of all officials, and produce the necessary aerial Protection that is available for the shores of our Country, if need be. Charge It forth in all official places! Make them understand, feel, and realize that this is a vital, important thing now!

We give praise and thanks that the Light is Its Dominion in America, in Washington, in New York, in Los Angeles, and that those fiendish communistic agitators are wiped from the face of the Earth forever. We thank Thee it is done.

Precious, Beloved Ones, I love you; and I thank and bless you for your joyous, willing cooperation. May your reward be limitless in all Its Perfecting Powers in, through, and about you, that will keep you so happy, so enthusiastic, and so buoyant that only the Glory of your Light finds expression at any time in Its ever-expanding Glory, in the supplying of every good thing that your world requires or that you require for use; and in your Power of Light called into action, there is no resistance or interference. Realize the powers of wealth and all of the Universe are at your Command. Accept it in its fullness, and may that accumulated wealth of past centuries be now released into your use in the Service of the Light, so that quickly may come into being those Blessings in America—your own Sacred Sanctuaries that will hold the people, ten thousand of them in each place, to live in the Glory of this Eternal Light; and I thank you.

CHAPTER VIII

April 26, 1938

DETROIT, MICHIGAN

Beloved Ones, may I hold you in My Heart tonight while I talk to you?

First, I wish to call your attention to the speed with which an attempted projection of disturbance was dispelled—how much more quickly than ever before in your experience before the Class! It is not surprising that before every Class an attempt should be made; but as you observe and see the effect of quick, sudden, dynamic Application, you will find It will apply in your individual requirements as much as in reference to the Class Work.

I want you to so much realize how really all-powerful your Application is; but do not let the ease and appearance of great peace, joy, and happiness cause you to relax in your Application. *It is imperative,* because that which we call the sinister force will often withdraw and apparently disappear to have you get off guard so it can drive in. This is not anything to fear or be particularly concerned about, except the guard must constantly be kept up.

You will find in this Class a mighty Impulse for the opening tomorrow. If you were to see how much, or shall I say how little the effect of destructive individuals is in comparison to what it was, well, about two and a half years ago, you would be certainly rejoiced. The effect of the radiation that they send out does not reach one-hundredth part the distance from that form that it did two and a half years ago. Today the destructive forces and quality sent out by every vicious individual is steadily and surely recoiling upon them; and when those individuals are held in the embrace of their own vicious creation, it will not be a happy moment. But the Law of Life is compelling it. It is not that anyone wishes it; but it is because no longer will Life tolerate this frightful thing of the destructive activity of mankind, which would have destroyed them.

There are several points I want to cover tonight. I cannot take as much time as usual, so don't mind if I go from one to the other rapidly in order to cover them.

First: Each time the opportunity of prompting occurs, it is because of the greater intensified vibratory action; and unless you are prompted, I am sure you are not aware of the increased requirement. You see, I am sure you do not, any of you, realize yet *the imperative need of keeping the attunement of the atomic structure up with the expansion of the Light within.* Now, please make a mental note of this and hold it before you, and if necessary write that sentence and put it up in your room.

You see—now let us cover this point: It might be well, if you do not mind, to put the whole paragraph referring to this especially, up in your room. We have talked an awful lot about harmony of the feeling world, the atomic structure; and yet, *the human obedience has not been sufficient to keep the needed harmony, for the atomic structure to raise its vibratory action with the expansion of the Light within.* That is the reason why, ofttimes, irritation temporarily disturbs individuals. It is so imperative! You do not see this from the Inner standpoint; therefore, unless you are prompted, you might easily fall prey to the human creations that always, of course, want you to fail. But I must tell you again, that you on the Staff here are in a very definite position, a different responsibility than the ordinary Student, because you are in the Heart Focus of Light that must necessarily be more intense than that without.

I would suggest in regard to the music, please withdraw your attention from outer, shall we say, technical requirements. I do not mean by that, you do not need to get your music in proper order; but if We are to bring forward the musical things that are waiting in the atmosphere about you to come forth, the *feeling* must be released within you from the constant feeling that, "Well, we must hold closer to the old outer method of technique." You prevent the Beauty and Perfection coming through if you have that feeling within you. I think you should have sufficient proof through this good Brother who understands so very little about music from the technical standpoint, and yet has been able to bring forth "Light of My Heart," which from a musical standpoint is amazingly correct.

You see, I wonder if you quite understand. At first you have to give the opening; and if the feeling is held to the outer technique of things, you cannot give the opening—or you would not give the freedom in the feeling for the Perfection of the Inner and more beautiful and perfect things to come forth. Therefore, I suggest each one of you who is working on music, hold yourselves in complete relaxation and readiness. Don't worry whether the thing is going to be correct or not, but let it flow; and then as it comes forth—and suppose in the first few weeks' work, or few months' for that matter, it is not just as perfect as it should be—it will give the opening to make the absolutely perfect come forth.

When you reach a certain point of continuous attention upon that, the Higher Mental Body will compel the outer to give the necessary obedience for this Perfection to come forth; but It would not do it until you come to a certain point, which I cannot explain to you in so many words because it is a matter of *feeling.* But you will find if you will do this, that everything will come forth with so much greater ease.

The outer world is no criterion to go by. It has failed in every blessed thing that mankind has tried to do, so why hang on to it? Branch out fearlessly and let the Power of the "Presence" have an opportunity. Do you not see, Beloved Ones, if this good Brother and Lotus had that feeling, or fear of what somebody was going to say or criticize them, where would they be? Right back in the condition where they started from. Therefore, *it is imperative that you compel your feeling to yield to the requirement of the Inner Activity.*

I must prompt you again on a greater consideration, dignity, and kindness to each other. Again I say it is all right to be happy and, as you term it, "kid" each other some; but watch out that it is always done at the right time. *Try to be gentle and kindly with everyone, even though they make mistakes sometimes.* It is getting more and more imperative because of the greater Forces that are being released; and if you will do that, I will appreciate it tremendously.

You see, our personalities outside are really of no consideration now in this Great Service that is being rendered, and in the tremendous change in the atomic structures of your bodies. You do not realize the rapid change that is taking action in the atomic structure of the body.

I wonder, do you realize—for instance, just take a seemingly little thing, like when you get a certain congestion which is so-called a cold in the body. It keeps the attention fixed upon the condition, and calls it back again and again to the atomic structure of the body, which is not always so good.

When the body is acting normally, it is the same way with eating. If you know a thing disturbs you and you determine to do it—well, if you have disturbance, is it not a lack of judgment in not refusing to take into the system the thing you know has been just a little bit too much for you?

Really, every one of you are at the point right now where you could control that as perfectly as could be, if you would just speak to your "Presence"—which would cause your Higher Mental Body to take command of all gastric action, take command of all mastication of your

went through the mill, and you don't have half of what I had to contend with.

Question: Is there any Call we can make concerning this stealing of military secrets by foreign nations?

Saint Germain: I think your general Decrees that you have been giving for the Protection of the aerial service and all that, is sufficient. Just keep pounding away at it. It has done tremendous service.

Question: Is it of any value to have a Dome of Light placed over the principal cities of the Country?

Saint Germain: It is a splendid thing. You see, I had not intended to say this, but I think I should tonight. The enormous work that is being done in the removal of entities from the Earth is removing the need of many things that I had thought would be imperative to do and to use, even yet, for and including the Shrine Class. But the Calls, and the Answers by the Legions of Light are—well, shall I quote Lotus in her explanation: "It is marvelous, stupendous, colossal!" It really is. I tell you, Dear Ones, you could hardly conceive of this, that humanity all this time could have been utilizing—could have awakened even to the degree that it has today.

You will never know—while Our Assistance and the Legions of Light and the Cosmic Beings', of course, is tremendous, yet this Outpouring of the Cosmic Light and this Wave that will flood again at the opening of the Class tomorrow (well, it really begins about eleven o'clock)—how much Work It is doing that would have been necessary for *you* to do in Application. Yet I urge you, under no circumstance let down on your Application for Protection and all that.

I want you to see how necessary it is when individuals of the outer world try to be dominant or vicious, and you just suddenly command that firm attitude—how quickly those people at the radio station smiled last night when that thing tried to drive in. They will, afterwards, realize you are people who are kind but know your rights, and it is absolutely correct. But all those things can always be done with a great and mighty firmness, and still nothing ugly or unkind in it. That is where the great Victory comes in—when they see that great calm yet unyielding determination, then their respect is greater than ever.

Don't have any concern. Don't have any fear of what individuals might be temporarily doing, but rather take the attitude: "*'Mighty I AM Presence,' You are in full Command of whatever the condition or*

accept It; and try to feel each time you contemplate It, a greater Confidence, Assurance, greater Power. It is the full Authority because there is no authority in the Universe outside of the Light from which all things came, because It is the Intelligence which is the Power of Light; therefore, It is Authority.

I wonder if you blessed ones know how much I love you; and when I see you steadily and surely gaining your great Victory and Freedom, oh, what a marvelous thing it is.

I suppose, My Sons and Daughters, I will have to be Granddad if Godfré is Papa, or I will have to be Grandpapa. I do want you to feel how dear every one of you is to Me. When I see you willing to give obedience and gain the expansion of your Light that has already been, it is a very wonderful, wonderful thing. You cannot conceive yet in the outer what that has meant within each one of you.

If you only knew these sacred hours that We visit together, how very sacred they are—that it is the Preparation for your Eternal Freedom from human limitations, and is the Command of all energy and substance. May I just remind you, then I must go: look through the ages, and that which had to come wholly through Inspiration or Inner Promptings, how, at intervals, these things came through so wonderfully and are such a blessing to mankind.

For instance, in almost every century there have been some things come through in music that held the Power of Healing. There is no question about it because they have produced results, and sometimes the most amazing. Therefore, think of the vast difference today. While as yet We must ask you to call forth from your "Presence"—but suppose, now this is just supposition, but suppose the Great Law saw fit to reveal Music—Words and Music—saw fit to reveal certain inventions that all the outer world would accept quickly and gladly, or whatever Life might see fit to utilize; and with this manner of Projected Words in Light, how all these things could be absolutely created and in readiness for use.

We have only yet given you just a fragment. All these Magnificent Dictations that have been dictated—do you not realize that it is only a fragment of what could come forth; but it is useless to give forth what mankind would not comprehend or understand. But I want you to feel how limitless is this great scope before you in the means of bringing things forth in this manner.

I could right now bring forth—give you the Words and Music and some instrumental Music

tremendous Application, but yet only producing partial results just because they did not know the whereabouts of the "Presence."

Look at the position the Messengers are in today, and all that has been done and accomplished. Why, there is no human source on the face of the Earth that has ever done anything like it or accomplished anything like it, and I say to you—here I am, going again!

I thought today this channel for the distribution of your compositions is the thing musicians in the past have worked for, for fifty years of their life before they got an opportunity to present it to the public. What do you think the composers of those days would have accomplished for the world had they had an opportunity of this day? Why, they would have swept the world in no time with the things that poured forth, because they would have had the encouragement—instead of the constant beating down—that would have given the open door for the great Music of the Spheres to come forth into action and use.

Mrs. Ballard: Talk about musical experience—I spent twenty years, and yet where did I get?

Saint Germain: But look! If I recall, it was in your third composition that you wrote as powerful a thing as was ever written for the harp—your "March Triumphal"—showing how it came forth with the ease of a breath. Do you not see, Dear Ones! Please, won't you feel here tonight you are in a position to be cared for—really no cause for anxiety—and the opportunity is here now to bring forth these things. Won't you love each other, and be happy and harmonious in the opportunity that is before you, and do these things. Why, it is a wonderful thing. It is marvelous!

I want to tell you, Blessed Ones, you would scarcely believe it, but in the Heart of everyone who has viciously opposed the Messengers, they have their respect; for they know even in their viciousness what the Messengers have stood up against, and have won that Victory; and there is not an ordinary activity of individuals in the world's walk of life that is anything in comparison.

Therefore, rejoice, oh, with all your Hearts. Take advantage of the opportunity, and make it bear such fruit that your garden will be filled with the Jewels from the Treasure-house of your "Presence" in all Its Rainbow Rays, and your Castle of Light decorated by the Rainbow Rays directed by your Higher Mental Body. As you saw the diamond under the central dome in the capitol in Cuba, how tiny that is in comparison with the Jewels within your own Homes of Light which you enjoy during sleep. Then you would say, "Well,

of the day is the most important thing now. After the Victory is won, then we can have lots of good times. Oh yes, I think you will be quite satisfied with all that will occur; but in the meantime, just go on in this great Service with a Heart full of rejoicing.

Oh, don't take the appearance world too seriously; only keep up your dynamic Application, knowing these appearances in the outer world have no power. With firm, powerful determination go on in that Service.

In order that your attention may be upon it, I trust that I will be able to cause to be done something very gratifying and far-reaching through the Exposition in New York, as well as San Francisco. Between the two We should be able to do a great deal in calling the attention of mankind to the Great "Presence."

Again I thank you. I must say good-night, and all the Love and Blessings enfold you. I call forth the Mighty Power of your own "Presence" through each one's Higher Mental Body to give you such Happiness, and the full, great calm Mastery and Feeling and Confidence of your Calls to release that Power of Light that gives you the Perfect Ease and Rest in the Victory over whatever confronts you in any way; and that the Glory of the Light, going forth from you, is the Victory, the Harmony, and the Dominion in your world.

The Beloved Masters Rex and Bob, Nada and Pearl, Mr. and Mrs. Rayborn, David Lloyd, Beloved Jesus, Nada, the Great Divine Director, Mighty Astrea, Victory, the Goddess of Liberty, the Queen of Light, and Oromasis all send Their very great Love and Blessings to you. Know that you are never out of Their Consciousness, that you may feel the full Force of the Blessing from each one of Them.

Good night.

and conditions that you will be able to govern yourselves in absolute happiness and harmony that makes it possible for Us to do the things We need to do. You have no idea what that would mean to you and to Us—absolute harmony maintained in your feelings, in your association, for six months.

I know it is not quite possible, unless you saw with Me from the Octave above just what all this means, but it is so vital! It is so important that I again plead with you: *don't let anything under any circumstance disturb your feelings* because, you see, We have gained such a Victory in spite of all that has had to be met, that if that can be done (and it was with those conditions), what magnificent Marvels would be accomplished with absolute perfect harmony, because it releases the full Power of the Forces of Light. But that has to be done over a sufficient period to get the momentum gathered.

I say this to you advisedly tonight: such a tremendous momentum was gathered for you individually and for the future activity during this Class, that I want you to realize that to hold and sustain the harmony in yourself, that none of that be requalified—We can do what We plan to do any time; and I can assure you, I shall delight your Hearts, every one of you, beyond your fondest imagination if you will do this for Me, because We are going into very definite action.

I will never forget this Class, and you see how absolutely powerless all of the vicious forces are. They have no more power than a feather in a gust of wind. The only slightest touch of anything was when the gathered projection of force was there to make the people sleepy, so they would not comprehend. That was cleared immediately, so it was a very marvelous thing.

You see, really, and this is why I talk about it again, when there is sufficient harmony within a focus, all those things can be transmuted into an activity of service. While their intent is wholly wrong, yet with the sufficient gathered substance from the human octave, We can always change that into a thing of Divine Beauty and Perfection.

Because of certain individuals in the room on Ascension Day, We thought it unwise to give forth certain descriptions of things concerning the Ascensions, but it was the most magnificent thing ever witnessed on this Earth since the height of the Second Golden Age! The effect over the atmosphere of America as those twenty-five ascended was the most powerful thing We have ever witnessed in the human octave, and of course it

This is what I want you to feel, because it cannot draw anything from your physical energy and strength. That is why, as you realize this, you will find yourself sustained abundantly with all the energy you require for any service you wish to perform, and that will change the whole thing within your bodily activity; and as you give it a little more attention, it will make it practically impossible for you to become tired or exhausted. Then in an emergency when you need to use more energy, it is always there, and you will feel no sense of tire or exhaustion from its use.

Mrs. Ballard: Can we use the Activity of the Canopy like we use the Blue Lightning?

Saint Germain: I was just going to say that. If you will be aware of that—for instance: don't feel that this is the least complicated when these various things are added, but just feel that the Essence from that gold forms a Canopy above your human bodies as you move before mankind. This would be a very marvelous thing for you, especially for your voices. That Essence would release into your vocal cords and would give you some of the most astounding things in your voice. It would give a liquid quality and a flexibility of the vocal cords that would delight you beyond words.

CHAPTER X

July 29, 1938

Los Angeles, California

How very beautiful it is, Beloved Ones, to see the happiness released from the feeling world, and to see the difference between today and a few months ago, when the activity released was more from the intellectual than from the feeling world. Since the first time that I called the attention, or your attention was called to having your feelings follow your direction, your Call, it has performed a very wonderful Service for each one. Today your feeling is arising, which means that We can intensify the activity as it goes forth harmoniously to render for you a Service that We have waited to render.

I wish you would all take particular notice of this, because in your feeling, as you know, is your powerhouse; and when your feeling gives complete obedience to the Requirements, then are We able to enter into definite Action that will bring such definite Results that you will see the Law of Life is acting literally, mathematically; for having come forth from Life, then Life must be mathematical in its

Question: Is there some Call we could give which we have not yet given?

Saint Germain: No. You are doing all right; and rather than change your Mighty Decrees into another form—you see, We are building a form, and that is why I would not change it, unless I should find it necessary to direct you. I would hold the Decrees exactly the same, as much as possible; then you build power and momentum in that specific thing. And the Decrees contain now sufficient energy, so far as giving Us authority from the human octave is concerned.

If once you saw and knew—for instance, you take in the Group Work: They have held month after month to the exact wording of the Decrees, and you have no words that can describe the momentum and power that is building up. That goes forth in the mental and feeling world and stands there ready for action.

Question: As more gather and by their attention add their assistance, then that will in an emergency rush forward?

Saint Germain: Yes. The Cosmic Light will utilize it in releasing Its Power to render the Service to the Earth. Aside from what individuals will receive from this accumulation, the need today of the Cosmic Light is bringing Its Action into the Earth

—for instance, as the Goddess of Liberty said, "that Light as of a Thousand Suns." That means a certain accumulated energy and force accumulated by mankind will be expanded and amplified by the Cosmic Light.

Question: This does not encompass our individual work, does it?

Saint Germain: Oh yes, the Cosmic Light takes up that momentum and renders Its Service. That is wholly—I would not say "individual," yet it is, in one way; then all the other activity will take place. But I cannot impress too strongly upon your conscious feeling, the absolute necessity of these Calls, the specific Decrees for definite things which you have been following very remarkably. For instance, concerning transportation, concerning communication, concerning industry, concerning the spy activity, agitation, and all that kind of thing—you have been covering it very beautifully; but the thing is in gaining greater momentum of that, rather than changing the Pattern of the Decree.

David Lloyd's Experience, to Me, is the greatest proof so far in the outer world of what a *gained momentum* is and means to the individual, groups, or mass. Now you will see how his momentum, power, and energy gained, because the human part of the

you everywhere. As you keep charging that into the feeling world, there is always more or less that comes forth during the activity of the day; but remember that you never expend more than within ten percent of the limit you call forth. You always retain at least ten percent. Now that means within a short time, aside from the service rendered for the moment, you would gain an energy and power that would be ready for any emergency. It would govern anything that concerned you.

Now I am saying this today because I want you to come into very definite action. I mean within your own feeling world. This is for your own selves especially, but gains that momentum and power just the same as David Lloyd did that brought such tremendous results. Then you come to realize that you are dealing with a definite power of energy, qualified all the time, which is producing definite results.

In the Precipitated Dinners or Banquets I did not call all this forth just on the spur of the moment; but knowing what I intended to do, in the Octave above was prepared, ready, that which I lowered forth into visibility for use. Not that We could not draw It forth instantly and directly, but We utilize the same Wisdom and Judgment that

Our Beloved

should be used in the outer world wherein *you do not use energy unnecessarily. Not that there is not plenty of it, but there is a balance in all action of the Law.* In an emergency there is no limit to the energy which can be used and should be; but if you have not gained it in your feeling world, then it would have to be one of Us powerfully charging and releasing what you had accumulated, small or great, to furnish the energy for that specific achievement. Of course, this We have done many times; but We want you to feel your authority, your responsibility to govern these conditions yourselves.

It is just the same in calling forth your supply of money or whatever it is—the same with the Students, many of them not realizing that they have not generated and gathered enough energy because they have not been steady enough in their Call and charging their world with energy and power of achievement. They sometimes marvel that their Calls are not answered more quickly. Well, it is because their reservoir of energy has been exhausted to a large extent, and they are not charging it dynamically enough to recharge it and gain the momentum.

So, in this simple explanation you will see how every move you make, everything you do can be turned into a definite Law of Life in its Victory over the outer things. It is as definite as anything in the world, the most practical thing, because the simplicity of the Law makes it possible for any person who wants to, to comprehend.

I think it would be very well—of course your constant contact with the Messengers and Myself makes it very easy, but keep charging yourself with the explanation of any question or point that comes up in the mind. Keep charging your own feeling world with the explanation, the revelation of all that is required in your stream of activity. Then if that is not quickly revealed clearly to you, many times just a contact of the Radiation of the Messengers will call it forth, and just like that the whole clearness will stand forth.

We are going into such definite Action that I want each one to feel their great ability, and each one to come to the rescue or assistance of another. If for any reason they are not quite harmonized, just each one refuse to give expression to anything less than the Perfection of anything you want.

One thing I never have mentioned, but I thought I should today. It is so easy for little feelings to get started. *If someone likes something and somebody else does not, well, give praise and thanks for that which gives them harmony in their liking of the thing; but don't oppose it*—because that is where, if you saw when an argument reaches the physical, how much that added upon people in the feeling *before* it goes into the outer expression, you would say, "Why, I will correct this now."

All should be a great happy, joyous, harmonious Action of the Law. One can be happy and joyous without getting too personal. That starts a feeling within each other. Some of these things sound very simple and unimportant, but they are far more important than you realize in gaining the great Victory of complete harmony within the feeling world, and it is so imperative. But you are so near now where you have absolute mastery and self-control—utilize every opportunity to gain that mastery. Don't blame anyone for anything, but just simply arise in firmness and simply say, "Now here is another opportunity for my self-control and mastery." It does not make any difference what the condition might have been or intended, but your self-control and mastery is of importance.

Please do not feel at any time any particular concern or disturbance at the more violent action of people who would seem to oppose. It means that that is just that much nearer the end of it. No one has any power to oppose this Work. No one has any power to oppose you so long as you are in accord and harmony with your Life. But discord, irritation, and disturbance in your feeling world is not in harmony with your Life Stream, which is Harmony, Happiness, and Perfection. So the moment something starts, just annihilate its cause and effect right then; for as I have said so many times, people think it is persons, places, and conditions. It is not. It is just a condition to be mastered, no matter what the cause of it is; and you, as the Heartbeat of your Life Stream, have the Power and Authority to do it. Try to feel this definitely and how important it is.

I tell you, Dear Ones, it has not anything to do with your world—what someone else does—but complete harmony within your feeling world is everything. There is no provocation justifiable in human contact to cause you to be irritated or disturbed; and don't, anyone, hold disturbed or irritated feelings within you, because I know it the moment it is there, but I try earnestly to help you dissolve it. So if you will let go of it, I will do the rest, or at least the most of it until you have the full Power to do it yourself. When you have gained this point of Victory—you have no idea how I feel, how I want to see you so quickly complete It.

I am never the slightest concerned if you make mistakes or slip sometimes. That has not anything to do with it; but if I see you begin to release feelings to each other, then I have to stop that because it would gain momentum and destroy definitely the purpose you are working for. Therefore, if I prompt you to give obedience, then it is so quickly dissolved, because I would not mention anything unless it was imperative to the full Achievement; but I do not want you to be delayed anymore. That is the great point.

If I did not know definitely you are at the point where you can go forward with tremendous power and speed, I would not keep after you; but I have to do it because we do not want to go fidgeting around here for months in doing what we could accomplish in a few days. Therefore, I rejoice so tremendously with you in that determination within each one to maintain that self-control and harmony.

In your joking about ———'s statement—harmonize your feelings and use the Violet Consuming Flame—that is really no joke, but of vital importance; and I really do congratulate you, every one, sincerely at the tremendous, in fact enormous Victory you have gained in the past three months. You see, *We never formulate any opinion on what the lips speak, but what is being released from the feeling world is the thing that is imperative to Us.* That is why it has not been so easy for you, because We saw acting, before you were aware of it, the things in the feeling world that are of vital importance. Once you watch and stand guard over the slightest intimation, well, the governing activity of the feeling becomes just as easy as breathing. The only thing that ever has made it difficult for mankind is the momentum they have in requalified energy; and remember, sometimes you have released through intense feelings just great quantities of energy. If that was wrongly qualified, then when it bursts into action, well, anything can happen. But your feeling world now is cleared sufficiently that with the determination not to let any inharmony act, I tell you in sixty days almost any marvelous thing might happen in, through, and about you. It is worth everything in the world.

Oh, when I think of it—We did not have anybody to prompt Us. No one was permitted to. Only when We had gained a Victory were We able to look back and see how joyful it was. But today, you, in having the promptings that are permitted these days and knowing the goal, well, then it makes everything so much easier, so much greater within your own grasp.

I really cannot tell you, Beloved Ones, how—shall I use the word—it is almost *incredible,* even in the slight intimation, the number of people that have determined and are calling their "Presence" into Action to be in that Class in Chicago. I question very much if the Civic Opera House will hold them.

Now notice again, you have seen what happened at the Shrine and the viciousness here. Well, think of the momentum of ten years. Just suddenly—like a punctured balloon—it lets go. Do you understand Me? Do you see what stupendous things are before you? Now this has actually taken place within the energy, within the substance of the feeling world there. Do you realize that that had actually built an activity in Chicago that held destructive forces toward the Messengers? It actually did. It had created a definite form, but today that form does not exist. You see what that means?

There was intelligence acting within that form because it went forth from individuals; then to see that dissolved, almost like you would draw your hands like that—the moment the people saw that, all opportunity within the legal action there was annulled. Then that released the feeling which allowed Us to pour the Rays in there to dissolve cause and effect of that which had been of ten years' standing.

Now, it is so within each one of you, no matter what would have been in the past; and of course, largely, all of you have had—with your effort and assistance—consumed what has been in your Life Stream. But in those who have not had the fullness of that understanding, don't you see how, unless they would understand the need of holding harmony in their feelings, well—everything, all the rest is so easy. It really is proof that in your Call to the Light all struggle ceases. Not that you don't have to be dynamic in your Calls up to a certain point, but the result comes by the Power of Light and with the ease of breathing. The Light is released and the other disappears, and that is so in all these activities. That was so in the releasing of those conditions.

You had been calling forth the Light, the dissolving Power; and when the right man was touched, all that momentum gained, rushed through and acted in and through him, producing the results you required. It is the same thing within yourselves as you call forth this Mighty Energy qualified for a certain Victory. When It has gained this Balance of Requirement, It rushes forward like that, and It is the Power of Light. It is just like a breath. It goes in and you find the other is dissolved. Once you get the feeling of that, you will have such instantaneous, powerful results, because the resistance of the human goes down and lets the Pure Energy of Life come forth for the rendered service.

You see, you have been going along quite easily, but in the Class radio work, the transcriptions, people are becoming interested. You have no idea—one person hears a transcription; they tell perhaps not less than five and often ten people. Then those individuals call the attention to two, three, maybe ten more. Do you not see how there is always infinite expansion. The transcriptions, the radio work in the Classes—why, thousands of people listen to those Class broadcasts. I mean by that, people who do not contact this Work.

Therefore I say to you, as the momentum gains a little more, you will find these people will come in with an acceptance, a readiness that will make an absolute demand for larger places.

The Great Law has seen fit to provide the great financial supply here that has made it possible for other parts of the Country to have this Work, which could not have had It without the supply released here. And not only that, but those from the West Coast have gone with the Messengers and have given great assistance with that supply in other places. I have been watching this very carefully, and it has been a very marvelous thing. The people of Los Angeles, I tell you, Dear People, have rendered tremendous service because of the assistance that has been given.

The Great Cosmic Light is the Governing Power of the Universe; and when the Life Streams of individuals come to a point of action wherein the Cosmic Light may act, and especially at the Call now of individuals, It expands so powerfully and so rapidly that there are thousands of people you never dreamed of today that have heard these radio talks and broadcasts, who are making their Calls to the best of their ability, silently.

Shall I tell you what it is mathematically? Over sixty thousand people since the beginning of the New York Class who have not contacted this Work in any way except through the radio, are making the Calls since you left New York. That, of course, is a tremendous thing, and only a small part of what will be. They are making the Call through having heard these broadcasts. You see, these transcriptions are going almost everywhere now, and they are reaching a balancing activity throughout the United States. That is the thing that We have been after.

Remember, your listeners to the transcriptions and the radio, I think We could safely approximate, are only one-tenth of those who actually hear it because they spread it to the first individual, and that one expresses it to two or three more; and it will easily average ten to every one who listens to the radio. When you stop to realize, it is a stupendous thing! And don't you see, when they are listening, they are quiet; they are not interfered with by anybody around them. Therefore they are more susceptible to the acceptance of it. That is why I have said a few things Myself; but where you keep it from being controversial in any way, or giving any attention to what anybody might have said, you are fulfilling the Law in the fact that they are harmonious; and if you don't say something that startles them, they are more receptive.

So you see, the need of wholly constructive activity is necessary. That is why in the Class Work—just leave it to Me; and if it is necessary, I will cause to be said whatever is necessary. But I feel sure We can hold wholly to the constructive activity now with such a power it will be a delight to everybody concerned, because We have a momentum now with the Students giving these Decrees.

Remember why I impelled the Messenger to be almost drastic—because they had not gained the momentum of the Decrees to go forth in the mental and feeling world. Do you realize the Power of that going forth now from—I should say actually that there are three hundred thousand

Students that are giving these daily Decrees. Well, it is an enormous thing when you start the dynamic Energy that is released. That is gaining, of course, every day. Then you can understand how this is steadily and surely becoming the Governing Power with these people who contact individual to individual. That is why Wisdom demanded that, in the coming forth of the Messengers, it had to be built on a firm foundation—therefore could not be done by advertising. This today has become the very *Call to Life,* the greatest advertising in the world if you look at it from that standpoint. Yet, this is not a form of advertising, but it is a form of reality which is the action of Life, of Light.

This has been a great joy. I want you to know it. My Heart rejoices extremely, for again much has been done today. Go forth in the great happiness that belongs to you. Don't let human beings or qualities or conditions deprive you of that great happiness. Oh, just go forth so happy and free, and just release that great joy and kindliness everywhere.

Now when I say that, don't think that I mean you need not be alert. Be so alert to the treachery and conditions about you that you don't lose that alertness in your joy and happiness.

Mrs. Ballard: Thank You for blessing "Your" own Home again with Your Presence.

Saint Germain: I do bless everyone here with all the Love of My Heart. Beloved Nada and many of the Great Ones join Me.

Mrs. Ballard: Will You charge into this Home another supply of Your Power to last us until You come again?

Saint Germain: Yes. It is Inexhaustible. You cannot be deprived of It in Its Limitless Supply; and with your adoration, great love to Us, and harmony maintained within your feelings, there is nothing required in the outer world that cannot be done. We are just as interested in your progress and your happiness and achievement as if—in fact, far more than if We were in physical embodiment here, because We see the Goal of mankind. We see your Goal of Freedom and *We* can well afford to be patient. *You* can well afford to be patient; and if something trips you up and throws you down, climb up and with greater determination go on. But because you slip once in a while, don't let it discourage you. Don't condemn yourself; but with greater joyous determination than ever, climb up and go on.

Never, never, Dear Ones, in thousands of years—while there is still acting the two extremes of conditions, yet never in thousands of years has there been such magnificent opportunity as is before you today in this great, tremendous Service.

I must go, and I thank you with all My Heart for your love and kindness. May the full Powers of your "Mighty I AM Presence" take command of you and your world, and Its Mighty Activity spread forth such a Power of Its Radiance and Happiness through you, that no one single thing will ever mar the harmony of your feeling world. That allows the full Power of your "Presence" to flow forth, produce Its Perfection, and hold Its Dominion in every single requirement with the power and speed of lightning.

Remember that you have Authority and Power in the use of the Cross of Blue Flame that is greater, issued in one of your Decrees, than all the physical activities of mankind put together. It cannot fail ever to produce the results you require, but It is the greatest Blessing against vicious individuals that can possibly be used.

All Our Love and Blessings enfold you always to your great happiness, perfection, supply of money, and all else you require for your great Service in the Light. I thank you and bless you forever.

CHAPTER XI

August 15, 1938

Yosemite, California

I greet you, Beloved Ones, in the fullness of that Joy which has been filling your Hearts here; and how much it means to you can be little estimated at this time.

If the variety of your conversation is a criterion of those who should talk, we should need a regiment here. However, tonight I trust you will be satisfied with Me. There is so much to be said of this most unusual place.

Since your desire is to know something about the cause of this valley, let us begin by stating that this end of the valley was the end of a branch of the great gas belts, and I mean by that, the upper one. About the position of the entrance to the tunnel as you drive through, was a place where a small opening from the gas belt beneath came through; but it was small enough that the pressure did not break the formation between the two gas belts, but added enough to this spur to release that terrific power, not of explosion, but of a rending power which lifted and divided the mountain at this point —making this not what you see today, but perhaps the most rugged spot (immediately after its formation) on the face of the Earth. This occurred, well, perhaps I should say was the *beginning* of the last cataclysm that changed the great surface of the Earth.

Question: Was that the cataclysm twelve thousand years ago?

Saint Germain: Yes, and during the first 1,200 years after this was made, it remained so tremendously rugged; then it began to fill in. About 4,800 years after that, there was a great tremor, an earthquake through this country which loosened parts of the walls—which you now see as these great boulders in the valley. That which still hung to the walls was loosened and started the greater filling in. You would be astonished to see how far down these boulders—as you see, on going up to Mirror Lake—filled in underneath where you are. That is nearly one thousand feet underneath where you are—from where the formation began to divide and come up; and the distance was less than half what it is now between the walls. You can understand then, by the shattering, what it took to fill in that which has widened the space as you see it today. Then the erosion began to wash down and fill in.

You will be amazed to learn that at that time, at a depth of approximately four hundred feet beneath you, it opened what really was the mother lode of California. As I have said once or twice before, engineers and people think they have found the mother lode, but they never have; for this was the only opening, or the opening to the place leading down to it. It did not come to the surface, but was opened.

Question: Then the feeling I had the other day—out here by the river—that there was a deposit of gold someplace around here, is correct?

Saint Germain: Fabulous! The vein at this point was fabulous; but you see—please note how very wise the Great Ones governing Nature are, to see that those veins are covered again before coming into the hands of mankind.

Question: Doesn't the placing of that amount of gold also partly account for the feeling of Purity in this valley?

Saint Germain: Exactly. I was going to say that is why you feel the great Purity and Charge in the atmosphere here, and why human qualities brought in have practically no effect upon the atmosphere of this place—and will not, because of the Radiance coming forth from that which has been opened up.

Even what has covered it since, does not hold within it the Radiance that goes forth; for once that has been opened to the outer atmosphere, the filling in or covering over is not of sufficient density—like the solid rock that covered it before—to hold in the Radiance that comes through.

Question: Is it desirable that that should ever be made available to mankind, or rather would it be more useful within the Earth as a purifying agent?

Saint Germain: There are places where the mother lode comes so much nearer the surface, so much easier of access, that if it is wisdom to tap it, I think other places would be used rather than this. But according to the harmonization of the mass of mankind, and were it possible to harmonize mankind quickly—which it is, if they would give enough attention to the "Presence"—then at a time not far off, there would be a great deal released, but not until an Ascended Master is placed over the government. This would have to be governed by the Ruler of America, or that which could control it; for it would be a good while before there would not be some who had not progressed, where it would be dangerous to let it be known. I mean from that, the Inner scientific inventions would come forth, making it absolutely impossible for mankind to deceive each other. The Inner motive of all will be known. Then they will see that there is no opportunity to excuse deceit; therefore, it will disappear.

When you see today how many Students have come into this Understanding and received such Blessings and evidence—and yet the first time their feelings are touched, crossed, or opposed, how quickly they will begin to doubt the Reality of the Dictations and one thing or another. For instance, when I brought forth in open Class the motives of Dave Livingston, there were about twelve people who, up to that moment, had great confidence; and when I told the truth about that, they immediately came to the conclusion it was the Messenger instead of Myself who was talking. Too bad for them, however. But it shows you, and that is why I prompt you, every one of you, and always have, *whenever something comes for your blessing and benefit, or correction of your motives or faults—if you are big enough to accept it and profit by it, how great will be the glory and blessings released.* But just the moment I offer corrections, and someone doubts that it is Me, or believes it is the Messenger, or refuses to accept it as their correction, then they are closing the door to the great blessing which would come forth—because, I tell you, there has never been a Dictation given that has not been given by the Ascended

Master whose Name is there. Anybody who doubts that should realize that this good Messenger would have to be a very wise Being to give forth all of this Instruction.

Do you realize, any of you—I think not even Betty herself—the thousands and thousands of typewritten pages that have been dictated since the Dictations began? I mean in your Class Work, not referring to those before the Messengers came from Chicago, but that have come forth since the Class Dictations began. You would be astonished beyond words if you knew.

For nearly two hundred years, perhaps it would be clearer if I said up to approximately three hundred years ago, down about the position of the entrance—no, it is a little farther than that: where the entrance of the Park begins, coming in from Merced, was the barrier that shut this valley off entirely from the outer world; and during the earthquake, the barrier was released. For approximately two hundred years before the white man came, the Indians considered this the most sacred spot in America, and representatives from every tribe were sent here to spend so many days within this valley.

Underneath what is now the Falls, over on this side *(left)* as you go out, oh, for a long period, was a crevice in which the air pressure formed almost like a human voice, and that varied in tone, until the Indians called it the "Singing Waters." Through that, one of the Ascended Masters giving Assistance to the tribe of Indians spoke to them. Those representatives gathered here, and that is why, when the discovery of America brought the advent of the white man, they found the Indians of this part of the Earth so completely at peace. It was only after the Voice ceased speaking to them and they stopped sending representatives to this point, that they became subject to the other vibratory actions which created discord and war between themselves and those that came into the valley.

I would not say definitely at this time as to the number of years, but at a future time this valley will become one of the most beautiful places in all your America; for it will become a Powerful Focus of the Light. You have heard of the sunken gardens and the various things that have come to beautify places. Here you will find hanging gardens—the fondest dreamer of beauty could not picture what this will become in its beauty.

Do you wonder tonight why you were thinking of the Secret Valley? You will remember the very beautiful Chinese boy that was brought there? Others have been brought since this frightful destruction has been going on; and Beloved Fun Wey will be the trainer of them, because those who were in direct line of that dynasty have been preserved and taken away.

Don't misunderstand Me in what I am about to say. I don't wish you or anyone else to feel any awe toward the Messengers or toward Us, but do you realize that this Focus which is here, is that which must hold the balance for the Earth? Because the Messengers are so humble and natural, which is quite right, do you understand then why there are so many Students throughout America that feel almost worship from within, without knowing just why that feeling is there. From their Higher Mental Bodies they feel the importance—which they are not able to express—of the Work the Messengers are doing, and of their importance to the world.

When you see very vicious individuals trying to destroy the Work of the Messengers, can you wonder that We feel, for the first time in the conditions of the Earth, that they should be removed. We, who have watched the progress of mankind so long, and now when the opportunity is here for mankind to be free, and quickly, then to think that there is any human being on Earth who has enough depravity—either from the past or present—in their being, by which they could be used against the Light! That is the thing! While We know they have no power, and you and the Messengers know that, yet that is not the point; but to think in a day of such great Light that there could still be those who could be reached to that degree.

Question: Beings with God Life within them!

Saint Germain: Yes, with still enough depravity wherein the sinister force could reach them to do this, or attempt it.

I am speaking now as we would discuss individuals and the qualities of attainment. Yet (now, don't gasp when I say this), because knowing what you do today, if everyone entered into the full sincerity of the present Understanding, you are enough to absolutely govern the direction of the force and currents of energy—through Our Assistance—to regulate everything in America! It might mean a longer period in its accomplishment; but I mean you, standing immovable in the Acknowledgment and Call of your "Presence" into action, by Our Amplification would make it possible to regulate the entire conditions of America.

That is what it means for a few individuals to stand unyielding in the Power of Light, knowing Its Power, knowing It knows no opposition, but with the full determination not to give any outer appearance of destructive qualities any power whatsoever.

Now, this is a very great tip to you all, individually. You do not realize yet, although We have said it and caused the Messengers to say it so often, that when you call the Power of the Light into action, It is the Power of the Universe and knows no opposite! Therefore, can't you see why all destructive forces have no power, so far as you as individuals of the Light are concerned. And when you as Children of the Light say to all destructive forces looking your way: *"You have no power! You are helpless!"*—don't you see how you release the Infinite Power of Light into those conditions, so far as your individual worlds are concerned; and they could not touch It, interfere with It, or affect It in any way whatsoever.

The reason I keep at you on these points, is that I want to get the full Feeling in every one of you of the Truth of this. You can become such an immovable Power that there is nothing in the world that could stand before your combined outpouring in your Decrees for any specific thing.

Now look, the Messengers today get answers by the hundreds, instantaneously; and the Students do, in their Calls to them for assistance. Therefore, isn't it proof enough that the Power is gathered, that the Power is there?

I was thinking tonight that in your enjoyment here, were you aware of all the suspicion that is going through the minds of individuals during the time you are here, you would indeed have a hearty laugh. The moment the Messengers are not in the activity of the Class Work, every conceivable idea gets going of what is being done and what is going on; so you probably will hear that you have had some great revelation or been to a Retreat or somewhere, or all kinds of reports.

Question: Well, could You fix it up so the story would be true?

Saint Germain: That seems to be one on Me, doesn't it? I might.

Question: That is hopeful anyhow.

Saint Germain: You know, since Mohammed could not go to the mountain, the mountain came to Mohammed.

Question: Could we not go to the Cave of Symbols?

Saint Germain: It would be so much easier to go by aerial transportation—I mean individually—than it would for you to drive the cars over the mountains. It would be very much easier and facilitate the matter of time greatly.

Question: We would like Your means of conveyance.

Saint Germain: You know, I took this good Brother under My wing once, and he still survives it; so you might all.

Question: You might borrow Chananda's plane.

Saint Germain: Still more convenient, I might produce one of My own.

Well, Beloved Ones, if you saw the achievement, and I thought tonight when you were talking about your early experiences, if you saw, Betty, since the Messengers were in your home in Miami, Florida, the enormous advancement and change—not only in the expansion of the Light within yourself, but the great group of Students, and all that has been done—why never on the face of this Earth was such a miracle, so-called, performed. This will give you great encouragement. You know that all sincere Application could not know such a thing as failure. Know the Light within you is expanding hourly and daily. You know it is only a matter of time—as we still have to use a little of it—until all your desires will be fulfilled. I am sure you can all still be patient until that is done.

As soon as you can all be taught by Beloved Leto to go and come consciously from the body, then it will make the transportation of your bodies from point to point much easier. Myself, I think that should come about so that in case you should have a sudden invitation, you don't have to fuss about preparation to go—you know, all of this packing and all that. You don't have to take that along in that case, because then you have your garments for use as you need them, and you might use the Violet Consuming Flame instead of a toothbrush. Your requirements would be very little.

Question: Just as soon as Beloved Leto teaches us to go from the body consciously, then the door is wide open to turn and perfect the physical body?

Saint Germain: Yes, the time would be so short until your bodies would be transported anywhere—I mean, you would be able to do this yourselves without assistance.

Question: Like Mrs. Rayborn projecting the Light Rays into her body?

Saint Germain: Yes. Only this will be much more wonderful, because you will be manipulating Currents of Energy while still using the outer bodies, while She did it from the Higher Mental Body to the physical body. You see, while you are still manipulating the structure of the physical body to become aware of these Currents of Energy, oh, it makes it just worlds easier and more powerful of action in drawing these Currents into the outer world. That is the reason—of course, I have not said so, but you should have realized My inference before this. In all My urgent Requests for obedience and for harmony, it must have had a very definite purpose. Now I am saying to you, that was one of the principal reasons I have urged this so much—to bring you all to the point where this could be done. But in everyone there must be a sufficient determination and self-control that when you are taught to go and come consciously from the body, you would not under any pressure misuse that Power, because when you enter into that, you will have certain Powers which you can use (but which you cannot use yet). Therefore, I am determined that I am not going to endanger any of you.

You are all at a point now where you could easily do this, but the feelings must absolutely be governed; and I urge you not to get your little prods out at each other, even in fun. It is all right when everything is harmonious, but when someone is a little out of harmony, then that prod gets a little too severe; so don't take advantage of it, else it acts at the wrong time.

It is wonderful to be happy, a most marvelous thing; and really you have not any of you, I am sure—outside of the Messengers—released such real happiness from within your feeling world as you have done on this trip here. That should be great, great encouragement to all of you. It is really wonderful. You might think that at other times you were happy, but this is a deep Inner Happiness that is magnificent.

Do you know why this seems so much more beautiful to you than ever before? Because, of course, the season is more beautiful; but still the more noticeable change is within yourselves, because there is steadily growing greater and greater harmony, greater and greater self-control and governing power of all energy. I know words don't convey it; but *if you just really realized how quickly could come the Glories of all your Hearts desire, by complete harmony maintained in your feelings,* I am sure there is not one of you that would not do it in spite of anything.

We have watched to see the effect of the *Ascended Master Light* upon individuals, and it is all and more than We had hoped for. It is bringing back a confidence in the Dictations. These vicious, silly reports spread their disintegrating forces so far among mankind, and It is correcting it very rapidly.

These individuals who have turned so vicious—it is just because they want to have the freedom without giving obedience; and in most instances it is simply because they do not want to let go of the sex desire. Whenever they do not want to let go of the human sense desires, whatever the source may be, it is because they have not comprehended that in entering into the Light, all the Light holds is given into the use of the individual.

You know, when things pour forth so rapidly, the tendency of mankind is to take so much for granted, not being grateful enough to release the powers from within themselves. There is evidence before the whole world today in the activity of the Messengers, that should satisfy the most exacting. If they would stop to contemplate the enormous amount that has gone forth in the Books and the Magazine, in the perfection of the Illustrations, and the Music that is going forth, and all that kind of thing, which no one can deny is beautiful and magnificent even though not the Perfection that will later follow—still is it so far in advance of the Perfection thus far that anyone with half an eye can see that it is more than human.

The rapid activity of the Classes has held the Students in an exalted vibratory action. Just for a moment contemplate with Me, will you: Suppose the Students—now we will take it after the second Shrine Class—suppose the Messengers had given one Class a year in Los Angeles, one Class a year in some of the northern cities (San Francisco or Seattle), one Class in New York, one Class in Philadelphia, and one Class in Detroit. How many of the Students do you think would have held steadfast to the Light? Just about ten percent of what you have today!

Think of it; but that is why We kept you moving

so rapidly from one point to another, to sustain the Vibratory Action that was established there. I can never tell you how deep My Gratitude and that of all the Ascended Ones is, for your willingness to forget yourselves and give that Service, because it has meant the great number. Remember, out of those six hundred thousand Students that We have referred to today, there are something over four hundred thousand that are I think sufficiently staunch and loyal that if necessary they would arise as one to your defense. Now, that is something to contemplate. When two people can pour forth in less than four years that Power and Radiance of Divine Love to produce that, then it is something worthwhile considering and contemplating; but this is actually true, physically speaking.

Now then, just contemplate for a few moments what this means to yourselves. I want all the Staff to get this clearly tonight, because the thought of the Students never goes to the Messengers that it does not include the Staff these days. I want you to understand what that means to your assistance in their Call for your Happiness, Blessing, Supply, and Perfection. It should be of the greatest encouragement to each one of you, and the greatest joy. No other group on the face of the Earth has ever had that offered them. Never! And now mind you, in the former ages of Perfection—even great Perfection—this was not done.

In those ages it came through purely individual Application, amplified by the Great Ones; but still there was never such a thing known in the history of the Earth as the condition that exists today in the Students' Work for the Class Work, for the Staff, and all that goes to support the Work. There never was such a thing ever known. And to have the body of Students (I am referring just now to those I mentioned as dependable, say four hundred thousand) in every Class pouring forth from all parts of the world their Call to the "Presence" for Light, Divine Love, and Blessings—don't you see, never in the world was such a thing done!

The thing is, they are doing it joyfully and willingly, although they are not comprehending but a fragment of what this means in their Call; still is it giving Us and all the Great Ones the opportunity for amplification that has been the need throughout the ages.

Question: They do it because they want to.

Saint Germain: Exactly. To force somebody to do something, is no good. You might have a temporary result, but it does not remain. Mankind has to do things because they love to; and if they realize their Freedom is coming, then there is the incentive and definite motive for doing something. But unless the Students understand that, they cannot give the willing, joyous Service and still retain within them the reason for doing it.

You see the intellect—oh, not always, but in most instances—has to have before it some more or less "evidence" before it will really let go and give over to the feelings the power that belongs to it. Few are able to say to the intellect: *"Now be quiet! Sit down now and behave yourself."* There are those who can readily do that; but most of the Students cannot say to the intellect: *"Stop that! I will have no more of it."* If they could do that, how easy it would make the rest. You see?

I am more than delighted; and oh, this trip has accomplished more than I contemplated when I found you were going to come here. Remember what various ones of Us have said: It is one thing to do a thing when asked, but to do the same thing without being asked is still another thing. Oh, what a wonderful thing, Beloved Ones, to—from that Inner prompting—want to do the thing that I might ask you to do in case of emergency. What a wonderful thing it is.

I appreciate very greatly your deep feeling of gratitude. I appreciate it very much. It will open doors that you never dreamed were there. So, let us all go forward tonight so grateful, so happy, so firm, so determined to manifest complete self-control of all feeling activity, that we give all that Life asks in the Harmony of Life to call forth Its complete and mighty Release.

I am very glad, Lotus, that you received the impelling force to stay over until Thursday morning; for it gives the opportunity for continuation of the Work that I am sure will make you all tremendously stronger and more marvelous in every way, in meeting the conditions of the outer world.

I would suggest that those who are largely taking care of the correspondence, to so regulate your time that at least every other day you have two or three hours to get out away from it and take your mind wholly off of it. You will find you will be able to do the work so much more easily and rapidly. You will do the same work; but don't allow yourself to be drawn too deeply into the vibratory action of those letters without getting away from it, because the pull is becoming tremendous and you get the full vibratory action of that force in those letters. So, I urge you, be careful; and don't feel you are neglecting the work in taking a little extra time—but that will always be; you will never run away from it. Please get this in your feelings because it is important.

Therefore, if you will do this, you will find you will return to the correspondence so much easier and keep yourselves wholly free from the vibratory action that is contained in those letters, because many are written by their own hand and carry a strong vibratory action; therefore, you must protect yourselves against them.

Every letter that comes there, is the Call which the Higher Mental Bodies of the Messengers receive. Now, that Call is always answered, even before the letters reach them. More and more, the Students are learning to call to the Higher Mental Body instead of writing; otherwise, there would be about three times the correspondence as there is today. It is fortunate their attention was called to it, but a great number of the Students are already doing this.

Question: I see a lasso of Light going around each individual.

Saint Germain: Yes, but be sure you don't consider that lasso going from your physical body. If you want to use that, see It taking place from your Higher Mental Body, but never from your physical body—because if you do, you form a physical connection from your body, which is not well to do.

Mrs. Ballard: Why can we not make a mass Decree

and establish a Focus to answer the desperate Calls of mankind?

Saint Germain: Lotus, I am sure you are inspired. That is very, very important; and I have been hoping for weeks some of you would conceive of that, because it is important. If you make the Call, it will be drawn to act within the heart activity of the Staff and assist in this correspondence, and to answer definitely these tragic Calls. Because of the conditions that exist, you will probably get more and more of it for some time because this unemployment situation is making it desperate for many of the people.

You have no idea, I tell you, Dear Ones—of course, you all know the human creation is always waiting to surge in; and the moment you begin to depend upon outside sources, that begins to surge in. You see how in this experience it did, and you will find it in the musical work if you don't watch out. The most plausible suggestion will be offered that will throw you off; and the moment you believe you have made a mistake, then you open yourself to further mistakes. But just as quickly as you take your firm stand with the "Presence" and say: *"There is nothing else. I am not going to accept anything else. 'Mighty I AM Presence,' You give forth that which makes me understand. You take command of me and see that I do the perfect thing!"*—in that attitude you would bring forth such Perfection, you would be amazed yourself. I mean this to anyone who wants to give it their attention, because I tell you, Dear Ones, your attention is the most powerful thing in the Universe.

You see, if mankind only understood that this is really true! As I am talking to you now and flashing these Words here, the Messenger seems perfectly normal and natural—and is. But the fact that he is able to receive It with such speed and accuracy—We could produce whatever We wanted in the invention and discovery world; but that is not important at this time. The importance is of getting this to mankind —and the protection of America. What good would the information do if you had to hold it in the Retreats for the blessing of a few individuals today? We could take you all there, as far as that is concerned, and forget the world; but that is not the thing. The need is for mankind, because they must have it or perish. That is why I frankly say to you, at the time the Messengers came back from Honolulu, I was almost at the point of taking them because of conditions that existed; and here, where We had attempted to formulate such a powerful Focus, such disintegrating work was going on that I was almost tempted to take them and let the world fight it out. Still, there was enough good acting within the great number of Students even then, that I thought it was worth trying it out; and since they were so determined, ready, and willing to make the effort, I thought, "If they are, I can too." The proof of it was, the Inner Prompting from their own "Presence" was the encouragement needed that We did go on—which has shown, of course, it was well worth it.

You see, until you get a Commanding Power built up by earnest, sincere Students, you cannot tell which way it is going to turn. You cannot depend on it—and knowing how through the past two hundred years I met that so constantly: I would lift up a group of people to a certain point and, in spite of all I could do, down they would go, back into their old vibratory action. Then there was nothing I could do but withdraw, but this is wholly different this time.

Question: How was it the Great Divine Director was never in human embodiment? Did He come into His present condition from the Second Golden Age?

Saint Germain: Yes. He held His Dominion and kept Himself free from the discord. There were others who also did that; but He had even then decided to render a Service to the humanity of Earth, which He saw beginning to take place then. Expecting it might go on for a great period of time, it gave Him the determination to hold steadfast, which He did with many others—and three others whom you will hear from, provided humanity is sustained in its present upward trend. Should They come forth, you will see very great transformation taking place in mankind.

Dear Ones, do you realize what it means to try to help humanity in almost all countries of the Earth, and to find that you had failed because of their disobedience—not that I had failed, not in a single instance, because I never did; but the objective had failed because of the unwillingness to give obedience.

Then you can surely imagine what My Feeling is in finding the response today in America also reaching out to all parts of the world. You see, it is like a great hub of a wheel, with the spokes reaching out to the various countries in the world. Think of it—those people having no contact except the Books, and yet rising within them is such determination, knowing the Right. All of it has made them very staunch and wonderfully alert.

But every person does meet the opposition, so-called, in the outer world, or that which tries to turn them aside from the Pathway of Light. If they are not strong enough to resist it, it means they are going to have to go through some severe experience until they want the Light more than anything else.

Now then, I think we have had quite a visit tonight. Again I say to you that not one of you is the same being that came into this room two hours ago. I think I hear some of you saying that you should like to see a greater outpicturing. So shall it be. Oh, you will find that I am a real Friend after all, and I surely am no myth.

Donald Ballard: You watched over us very closely coming up here.

Saint Germain: It is quite necessary sometimes. What is your desire, Don, in your plans for your flying activity?

Donald Ballard: I want to get as much time as I can between now and the Oakland Class, and at least get my blind flying finished, and get my license as soon as possible in case there is a need.

Saint Germain: Would you rather return after the Oakland Class and continue your flying before you go to Chicago? I want you both to be in Chicago.

Donald Ballard: That was what I had in the back of my head.

Saint Germain: I think it would be a wise thing to

do. I think from now until you would go to the Oakland Class, you would find generally very good flying weather. It is not so important for you to be at the Seattle Class; and I think if it is satisfactory to both of you, it might be well and a very wise thing to return and get in all the flying you can.

I would suggest that you devote whatever time you need to your flying, but continue very earnest study. Besides getting the rest you need to keep yourself in perfect condition for flying, I would put in very earnest, sincere Application and study. I think you would both make tremendous progress if you would do that—I mean in a very methodical way. Don't let any condition come in; but make yourselves give obedience to your study and time, just the same as you were doing the regular activity.

Donald Ballard: You mean in reading the Books?

Saint Germain: Whatever you think you get the most out of in study, but do not miss your definite Application.

Question: When we get our own plane, would You approve of ________ to take the responsibility of the ship?

Saint Germain: Oh, yes. You would want someone to do that until Don has had a certain period of flying experience, even if his training was complete—because, like everything else, you need to become thoroughly adjusted to every requirement. He would be a very splendid man, I think, in taking that capacity of action.

Few can realize really what determined Application means. Anyone could set themselves free so quickly if they would really just enter into and make that dynamic Application. Everyone needs more of it, because when one is up against the suggestions of the outer world—and I don't mean by that, too prolonged Application; but to give snappy and powerful Application two, three, four, or five times a day for ten, fifteen minutes is more powerful than too prolonged Application until one loses the power of it.

One day, people will find I am very Real. They were so determined up to that time, that the Messenger was the one giving forth these Dictations. They have changed their minds since, and I think they will still change their minds some more.

What do you suppose they would do if I were suddenly to come forth in My Tangible Body, even today? Some of those who have been so determined that I was a myth, wouldn't they be surprised! Well, they have to have the opportunity to disintegrate that doubt. However, that does not worry Me; and I see it is not worrying you, so we shall go serenely on our way. However, the hour is getting such that I think we should not continue reminiscing.

Tonight, Beloved Ones, the Currents have been pouring through, instead of the Violet Consuming Flame pouring up. That should mean a great deal to all of you.

My paddlings are not very severe. Now, Dear Ones, I must say good-night to you; and all Our Love and Blessings, remember, constantly enfold you, to your great Perfection. I say to you: *make your powerful, dynamic Application.* Most of you are doing it; but the rest of you, feel the need. Don't leave it to your "Presence" or Me to do the work that your Application is required to do. So much Application is required of each one to enable Us to release the Assistance that you would like to have. We cannot go beyond the bounds of that which your Application enables Us to give; so remember, it is important for you to make your dynamic Application in order to give Us the opportunity to do the things We would love to do for you.

Good night. All Our Love and Blessings enfold you, Beloved Ones.

CHAPTER XII

August 17, 1938

Yosemite, California

Greetings, Beloved Ones! It is with great Joy that I observe your enthusiasm and determination in getting at the verification of the Truth of the Light. I have asked all the Students everywhere to be patient until the vibratory action becomes raised to a point where certain Manifestations can begin to take place.

You are at a point where this can be done, but it will not be done as long as there is anyone not holding self-control and allowing criticism and condemnation to go through their feeling.

One who has not been attuned through the years cannot possibly comprehend what it means to receive vibratory actions through the atomic structure of the body. A thing may not be wholly uncomfortable and yet be destructive; but when a thing gives you joy, enthusiasm, and the great uplift, then you can be sure that whatever position you are in at the time, that vibratory action acts upon the atomic structure and you will have perfect results.

When the body is out of harmony through discord revolving in the feeling, there is certain constructive music that would produce a perfect activity within the vibratory action of the body, if it is attuned. Now then, the "Song of the Islands" is one melody that no matter where the vibratory action of the body is—the atomic structure—it will take hold and raise and bring the body back into attunement. It is one of the very few melodies thus far that will perform that service for the structure of the human form. There are other melodies, after the body is brought to a certain attunement, that will take hold and act—probably not so powerfully, but similarly. That is why people who pose as an authority in music, not understanding these laws, will ofttimes and do constantly defeat their own purpose, their own achievement.

If you are to have the Blessings which come through this, I tell you if you will trust Me and give the obedience necessary, you will see such things as you never dreamed existed in the world.

I feel now we must put aside all childish foolishness and go into action; and when I speak the truth firmly to you, don't think it is in criticism of anyone. Now notice: when a harmonious force is denied action, then the inharmonious force will find an opportunity of action, because something must act. Life is perpetual motion; therefore, a force must act. And if it is not a harmonious force, then it is very apt to be an inharmonious one.

It is the Great Divine Director's Desire and Intent to bring forth a mechanical action through which the attunement of the physical body can quickly be brought into absolute adjustment. Now that means not only the atomic structure of the body, but the vibratory action will cause the spine and the bone structure to come into perfect position.

If you understand that the Light Pattern of the body can never be changed, and that for instance, the spine that gets out of order comes not from abnormal physical positions so much as an activity in the feeling world—that causes the abnormal position. Now for instance, one can sit slumped in a chair—well, that is not from an outer thing; that activity comes from within the feeling world, which causes you to slump. If the vibratory action through the feeling world was acting normally at all times, the spine would stay straight and in perfect condition—even when you are lying down in bed, you would not curl up. That is the abnormal condition in the feeling world that produces these outer effects. You would find that the individual with a normal action in the feeling world would lie perfectly straight in bed, either on the side or on the back, and there would not be the inclination to curl up in abnormal positions.

Now, for instance, the medical world will say to you, "Because of habit you have produced an abnormal condition of the spine." That does not come from outer habit. It comes first from a cause in the feeling world that causes those positions. Therefore, the cushions between the vertebrae in mankind are constantly moving. The cushions between the vertebrae of the spine are not such that they would come into an abnormal position without an activity within the feeling world.

Therefore, I say to you, every physical condition that exists has its cause within the feeling world, whether it is an abnormal position of the spine, the bone structure out of position, or whatever it is.

Now, I want to call your attention—perhaps some of you have heard the explanation; but the first patient that this good Messenger had in his experience of healing was one in whom the muscular contraction drew the left hip right out of place. Now let us understand the cause. Because of the abnormal sex activity of the individual, the psychic forces through the feeling world were acting upon that individual; and when he resisted that, the psychic forces would, by the viciousness due to disappointment, cause that muscular contraction from the feeling world that drew the hip out of place.

Question: Just because they failed to gratify that desire?

Saint Germain: Exactly. These are conditions—if mankind understood, they would be able to free themselves at once. From the time he laid his hand over that hip, which disconnected the psychic forces from that muscular activity, the patient was well.

Question: Did that come from this embodiment or another?

Saint Germain: That was from this embodiment.

Question: It does not necessarily have to be this embodiment, does it?

Saint Germain: Oh, no. So many of the causes of things are from past embodiments. That is why I say to you, Beloved Ones, why do you think We would day after day, month after month, implore the people to use the Violet Consuming Flame? Because It will release mankind from those conditions.

Now, when you stop to consider that the human cannot produce the Violet Consuming Flame, but you call your "Presence" to produce It—which is all Wisdom, all Power, all Love—don't you see, whether you were conscious of It or not, if you asked It to be sustained, it would be but a comparatively short time until everything would be dissolved and consumed from your feeling world that had been the means by which the sinister force could reach in and touch any one of you at the most unexpected time. That is why I have asked these things.

Question: When all is said and done, all cause of discord is psychic. The minute there is any discord, there is an intrusion on the emotional body.

Saint Germain: Dear Ones, will you just listen to that, please. That is absolutely true. There is no discordant activity that is not an intrusion into your feeling world by the psychic forces. You see? Now, it is nothing to be scared of. It is nothing to be disturbed about; only, if you understand what is acting, then you will be firm in holding your self-control and be prompted the minute something discordant starts to act. Then you have your signal that it is a sinister thing that is undesirable and must be dismissed. You have absolutely within your own grasp all that is necessary to dismiss any disturbance or sinister thing—whether it is projected at you, or whether it is individually within your own accumulation, or whatever it is.

Since you came here, so much more—I mean by that, so much greater speed of accomplishment has been done than I had even expected, that I am speaking this way today; for I do want so much to have definite, firm, powerful action now in the things we can accomplish. When We have the Power in Our Hands, and the Wisdom, why go on just in a halfway manner when We can enter into the full Power of Action and give this great Blessing that is so needed—not only that, but draw the great Perfection forth for yourselves as well.

Question: Cannot each one with firm determination make the Call to You and the Great Divine Director, the "Mighty I AM Presence" first, to do now whatever is necessary to take the last fragment of the human out of everybody, and replace it by the Ascended Masters' Obedience and Self-Control to provide whatever is needed this moment?

Saint Germain: That is all right; but you see, so little remains within the feeling world of each one. *The Call is all right; but unless the individual makes conscious effort at self-control, it won't do it. We are always ready to give assistance, but We cannot do it when there is not the willing obedience in the determination to hold self-control.* You can clear away everything within the feeling world of the individual, and in the lack of self-control they can begin to generate more and more right away. You see?

There is always the effect remaining, sometimes a short period after the cause is cleared and consumed, because that is in the force field around the Points of Light in the physical structure; but that of itself would have no effect upon the individual if they were determined in their self-control. That is why I have said so often, you cannot have Perfection without the determination to consciously hold self-control within the outer activity of the individual.

Now, just take it, for example, among yourselves: when you are all in a very happy state, you can say things to each other and it does not have any effect. It is just a happy expression. But you take people when they are a little out of harmony, and you say the same things; then it starts a furious feeling within them. Now, that is the lack of self-control. You see, when everybody is happy, things roll off; but when they are not, they don't. Then it begins to act and revolve in the feeling world.

I say to you, it is wonderful to be happy; but you can be happy *without* saying and doing things when you are not in a happy state, as it has its effect in the feeling world of each other. So I think you should use discrimination. Don't say things that could be construed as unkind to each other, because in those unguarded moments you start the disturbance again.

Question: To some degree, if we say the thing, we are responsible if we stir the other fellow into a discordant feeling.

Saint Germain: It does not make any difference whether that thing is *intended* or not; if it actually does that, you are responsible for stirring them up. You see?

Oh, we are steadily and surely getting at the understanding of this. I am sure everyone will hold such perfect self-control they won't do those things. But notice now—here are the two conditions: One is in the happy state and continues to say things that could be construed as unkind. The other person, for some reason, is not just in a perfect state of harmony; then that thing strikes through into the feeling world. Well, the two conditions are acting: One should not have said it; the other should have controlled their feelings. So both are making themselves a part of the inharmony in the feeling world.

These are things that are acting; but unless you understand them, don't you see you are helpless before them! That is where *self-control is the most vital thing of all qualities in the Universe.* You cannot have Perfection as long as you refuse to give obedience and hold self-control of your own feeling world. That is why many times people have made Application sufficiently dynamic and have produced wonderful results, but they have not held the self-control within their own feeling world. It seems almost incredible!

For instance, I call your attention to Mr. Ballard's experience with his associates in Los Angeles—before his experiences began in northern California. You do not know these people—as far as I know—but when they came to him, asking for money, and he would not "dish it out" to them, their feelings turned to hatred against him, and they spread every vicious lie imaginable. One man was on his knees to this good Messenger repeatedly as long as he got his way; but when Mr. Ballard would not give him the money he asked for, he turned bitter toward him and his Work.

Those people will reap what they sow—it cannot be otherwise. If they do not do something to correct it, they will come into the next embodiment in a far worse condition than ever. They won't find you blessed ones to vent their venom against, but it will be some other condition.

Question: Will this instrument that you just

referred to, that the Great Divine Director wishes to bring forth, will that do for mankind something similar to the one on Atlantis which they used on criminals?

Saint Germain: Yes. Within a few minutes or an hour or so, it will bring the Perfect Balance of the atomic structure of the body. That means the adjustment of the feeling world.

Question: That would be the person making the declaration?

Saint Germain: Well yes, because of the change in the Cosmic Activity, which is setting aside the destructive free will; then you can do things which would not be permitted before. You can so decree while this is taking place that it will be permanently sustained within the individual, thereby rendering a service which has never in the history of the Earth been permitted before; but the Cosmic Light is making it possible for this to be done. The Free Will of constructive activities has not been set aside; so, it will be, so far as the destructive qualities are concerned.

Question: Are not mankind mostly hypnotized; and when they are hypnotized to a certain point, they cannot cut themselves free without assistance from without?

Saint Germain: No; but as the destructive free will

is set aside, that in itself will be a great release to mankind. Now, notice this carefully: Any condition that has become a habit within an individual has, to some degree, what you would outwardly term a hypnotic influence, because it is involuntary action. The destructive accumulation of mankind has caused not only pressure, but this hypnotic effect upon the whole mass of mankind; and until their attention was called to the "Mighty I AM Presence" and the use of the Violet Consuming Flame, mankind had not a chance on Earth, or anywhere else, of getting free.

Notice, Blessed Ones, how really tragic it is. As long as the Violet Consuming Flame is not understood and used with dynamic Power, the accumulation builds and builds from one embodiment to the other. I do not mean between times, but whatever has been built in one embodiment stands there. It has to remain, waiting for the individual to come again; then it enters into the feeling world of that individual, because it is their own creation—and think what that is, to build for a hundred embodiments! Think of it, Dear Ones. Then think what this Understanding means to mankind today!

Why, Dear Ones, it almost makes one weep with gratitude that Life has brought forth such a clear, definite, magnificent Understanding of Life—

simple, yet Majestic and All-powerful. Why to think, in Our Attainment We had to, by sheer power of a determined will, call these things forth—why, with such determined effort that you could not imagine. You do not know what it means today, because everything is coming to you with such ease and such assistance.

Why, think! Think of My constant Promptings—never before in the world permitted. The Great Divine Director in His firmness will not give further Promptings; but when I know that with every one of you it is possible for you to hold that self-control, and in your Calls release from your "Presence" the Invincible Power of Perfection, I take upon Myself the Responsibility of giving you additional Promptings if your actions are out of order from the Divine Law.

I tell you, Dear Ones, I presume I ought to correct it a little for you. We have often talked about intellectual vanity. As I observe it more and more, it is really a sinister intrusion from the psychic world that utilizes that to sidetrack mankind. It is not so much within themselves.

I tell you, Beloved Ones, if you were to see how We have stirred the depths of hell. This Light, this Knowledge has stirred to its very depths the power of all destructive forces; and it had to be, because they must be dissolved and consumed. But you two Precious Messengers, you will never know until your Ascension what you have stood against. Now, not that you should ever be off guard, but it will be so much easier. Try, Beloved Ones, to comprehend what the dissolving and consuming of the war entity of the world means. Good Heavens, never in the history of the Earth has such a thing ever even been contemplated by the Great Ones of the Light!

Question: In doing that, You have taken from the sinister force its most vicious weapon.

Saint Germain: Exactly. Of course, if you could openly—but I do not think it wise yet, but as soon as it seems advisable, I will let you know—if these great Groups of Students could issue that Decree that all abnormal sex desire be dissolved and consumed from the experience of mankind and its accumulation of the past, I tell you, mankind would be released from more than any words could ever describe.

Question: We did give that Decree.

Saint Germain: Yes; but it stirs the fiends so tremendously, I think it is not wise to do too much of it yet. Always in your private Decrees you can do that. Oh, you have no idea the fiendishness that it stirs within individuals, some of them.

Question: Things like the war entity that we have

consumed, they can never come back again, can they?

Saint Germain: No, I do not say that they could not. It is just exactly like the conditions with an individual. You can have dissolved and consumed every vestige; yet, you can start in and by the lack of self-control rebuild that again. But of course, it would not be anything like that which it had been, because that is the accumulation of the ages. Now, this accumulation of the present would be but a fragment in comparison with the vast accumulation of the past.

This is the point with you: because you are the Heart Focus of this, it must spread out to others. But the reason I am stressing this now in this vibratory action today is so you won't forget it. Remember, you are calling forth ten, twenty, forty, maybe fifty times the energy that you were able to call forth before. Now then, if you requalify that by the lack of self-control, don't you see, then you would be building that many times more rapidly than you were able to build in the past? Because of the lack of understanding, it was just a condition of forces acting.

Question: Now these things can be done more quickly.

Saint Germain: Yes, it would if it was allowed to act; but since these Decrees are acting for the continual dissolving of all human creation, then it will prevent the starting of the accumulation of that again. That is why in withdrawing all power, energy, substance, and money from these destructive individuals, then it is just like you were gathering that up and preventing any further accumulation of that particular thing—because, you see, individuals who want to influence or propagate conditions that build for war, when you withdraw the money, energy, substance, and intelligence from that, then you have withdrawn the power that enables them to accumulate. While it may sound like a simple thing to you, I tell you, Dear Ones, you have no idea how far-reaching it is, because that gives Us the opportunity to take it up and amplify it. Don't you see, We cannot do a thing for your world, We being free from it; it is the people in this world in the need and requirement that must make the Call for Us to do the things that We can do—*but We cannot do it without the Call.*

Question: Even a few calling with great intensity do not completely answer for the Call which should come from each one?

Saint Germain: If We could—I don't mean this in numbers, because We have to be careful; it is rather quality or volume. Now, you take the whole mass of humanity, and you take fifty-five percent of them.

That would give the balance which We require. But at the same time, We do not require that fifty-five percent in *numbers;* We require it in *volume of energy* released. For instance, as soon as We have six hundred thousand who are earnest, loyal, and determined, I believe today as I see it, that sufficient volume would be released to hold that more than fifty-one percent, perhaps fifty-three percent of the volume for the whole of mankind. Do you not see how it is a magnificent thing beyond any concept of mankind in the world, to think that volume could be released by that number for the whole of mankind? It is a stupendous thing! But the Great Law of Life knows *this is the last opportunity for the Earth;* and unless the Victory is won this time, well, the Earth will have to experience the conditions, and the Earth would largely become barren.

Question: Cannot we consider destructive individuals the same as we consider discarnate entities, as to free will now?

Saint Germain: Yes. Don't have any qualms of conscience, Dear Ones. When an individual has become wholly destructive, it would be a thousand times better to make the Call and have them taken out of the body and stop that accumulation. You cannot destroy Life, but you can stop further accumulation of that destructive thing that is causing that for them.

Of course, I understand thoroughly that those poor unfortunate creatures have believed the old foolish idea.

Question: If each one of us would, three times a day, call to the "Presence" and the Great Ones to release the maximum quantity of energy to us, so that we could pass it back again to You, would that not take care of that?

Saint Germain: No. I would not attempt to do that, because it is too dangerous. One might do it for a time; then you might be off guard. I would not attempt it. Anyhow, it is not quite the correct thing, because mankind has to make the effort. You cannot just do a thing for someone—the Law of their Being is demanding effort upon their part. You can make the Call, that is all right; but leave it to the Great Wisdom and Power of Life to render the Service. Their own Life Stream has to have the expansion within Itself from their own Call.

I know you will all rejoice with Me when I say to you, I have never in three hundred years felt so encouraged, so rejoiced at the possibilities of achievement, even with that which has already been achieved.

Question: Can we call forth a Temple of the Great

Silence in Yosemite, into which You can focus Your Power?

Saint Germain: Dear Ones, don't you see—no one can possibly conceive what your Call to Life might produce. Don't you see! Not even We might, for the moment, know just what that great earnest, intense Call to Life might produce to bring into outer manifestation. How can you know unless you make the Call? Even if you did not find the outer manifestation within a certain scope of time, still would that Call, having gone forth, produce results beyond your fondest imagination. Therefore, don't hesitate ever to make the Call to Life—which is your "Mighty I AM"—for any of these things that you conceive of. Don't you see, Dear Ones: from the Great Law's standpoint, you cannot conceive of a thing in the intellect that would not be possible of attainment. You cannot do it; it is not possible.

Question: Let us make a written record of this while we are on the grounds, in full, specific detail; and will You focus the Unfed Flame within that to be maintained here forever?

Saint Germain: We have already established the Unfed Flame here. We established that the other night. It would become visible when that is established.

Question: When we look at "The Fire Fall," that

must be a symbol of something. Could it stand for a symbol of gold in this valley?

Saint Germain: It is a threefold symbol: first, of the radiance of gold underneath; then the Purification by fire; then it represents the Unfed Flame in Its Fullness. Always qualify it as that, as you observe it.

Don't you see there is no condition that would be for the perfection of mankind, that would not be possible of achievement. You know, sometimes when Life chooses to become the operation of a place, that place is sometimes offered for sale; and Life, being the abundance of all the money supply there is, would naturally produce it for the purchase.

Again we come back to the same old point—why the absolute harmony is needed. Then these things can so much more quickly come about.

Let Me say this to give you greater assurance: In the momentum that has been gained in your Calls to the "Presence," it makes it possible, wherever your bodies are, many times to utilize the opportunity to release a power of vibratory action into the environment to do the things We wish—unbeknown to yourselves. That is why many times it is important to have your bodies on the ground where We wish to do certain things. That was why it was necessary to go to Honolulu, and why it is necessary to have your bodies at certain points.

There is not one person who is the claw of the sinister force in the attempt to oppose this Work, that does not know in their Heart that We are Real, because they have seen the manifestation and they know the human could not produce it. Therefore, regardless of what might be said outside, they know *We are Real;* they know *We are the Power* with whom they are dealing. Therefore, they are always afraid of an invisible thing.

Question: Should we add to that Call the Decree to not only reveal, but to awaken the American people into action to the things that are revealed every day?

Saint Germain: Yes, by all means. Arouse them into action against it. You see, in all this Work, now what you need to do is to call all this into action, because it is *action* now we need to reveal a thing. Without action it would be only a fragmentary part; but awaken, arouse the people into the defense of America and themselves. The conditions that have existed so long have put the people into this sleep; but you would be astonished if you saw from within, how fast the awakening of the American people is coming about by these Decrees going forth.

Some of the Students cannot see how practical

We are, and when We get too practical they think there is something strange about it. Someday when I begin to come forth in My Tangible Body, you will look at Me many times and wonder how I can be so practical and natural in the outer world. You will pinch yourselves many times to make yourself believe that I am other than yourselves. That is the Reality of Life, Dear Ones. To assume what you are not is foolish, but to prove to the world the Law of Life by your actions is the greatest thing in the world.

I trust I can get you all to see and feel how, when you depend wholly upon your "Presence," it so transcends anything that exists in the outer world that there is not any comparison; and you don't have to use outer means in order to produce this Inner Perfection. In most instances it interferes instead of helping, and that is what all must understand. The Inner does not need the outer, but the outer surely does need the Inner. That is how in all your production of this Work it is wholly different from anything that has existed, because the outer has not reached an anchorage sufficiently; and as long as it begins to reach back into the outer for the assistance (the technical achievement of the outer world), that, because of the conditions that have existed, keeps drawing the attention back—instead of going to the "Presence" where it will produce greater and greater Perfection.

You see, the world has drawn itself into the limitations and conditions that exist by giving its attention to outer things. In dividing your attention from the "Presence" to that achieved in the outer world, you are more inclined to draw into the achievement of the outer world than the "Presence," because of your attention being so long fixed there.

I tell you, you have no idea yet of the enormity of your *attention.* It can bring you into Perfection or drag you into oblivion, it is so powerful. You see, this is the point: There is no outer, technical Perfection that can take the place of the Perfection of the "Presence." Now, the "Presence" can bring into action technical Perfection, but if the attention is fixed only on the outer, technical methods instead of the "Presence," then there will be no outer Perfection. *The "Presence" is first.* Everything that exists in the outer world had to come from the "Presence," but the dividing of the attention between the two in the present state of mankind is not condusive to the complete state of Perfection.

For instance, in your music when you strike a certain harmonious vibratory action, then you will be able to call forth—now, take this one piece as an illustration, the "Song of the Islands." It produces a *general* harmony. In order to call forth a *specific* harmony, the general attunement of your physical body and the brain structure needs to be brought to that certain attunement; then when you call forth a specific thing, don't you see, the channel is crystal clear for that specific thing to come forth. You would find it becoming just as definite and accurate as if you put down a row of figures and got an exact result.

In music, in art, it is all produced the same way. If the instrument, which is the body and brain, is not in a certain vibratory action of harmony, then if you call forth something that is specific you are very apt to have that colored by the vibratory action that remains there that is not perfect, not in full harmony. Therefore, you cannot call a specific thing there until you have reached a certain attunement by a general activity, which this music produces; then you can call forth specific things and get them uncolored by the vibratory action there. The body structure should be brought up to where all is in balance, before the specific thing is focused.

Question: In orchestrating numbers, I imagine a great deal of work could be done in balancing up the tonal quality of the instruments to put a healing quality into the music. For instance, certain types of instruments produce vibrations that are not wholly harmonious, and other instruments produce tones that are much more harmonious.

Saint Germain: That is the training you are receiving now. You will draw that quite clear into the outer consciousness and activity, because that is where you will be able to produce some very astonishing results. When these begin to come forth, you will probably receive some very fascinating offers; and when that comes, take your stand in the Light.

You don't realize, Dear Ones, how the outer world is craving this Perfection, which they know is being made manifest. There are already individuals who, if they dared, would offer this good Messenger millions of dollars to give them certain things; but they know they dare not do it.

You have a little evidence of how there is not anything in the world that could not be brought forth as We are able to flash these Words to the Messenger. Don't you realize, Dear Ones, that there is not one thing in the world of invention, discovery, or anything else that could not be brought forth? For instance, in the attunement of the music which you are being prepared for, don't you see that if it were necessary and you were not bringing it back clearly, I could prompt you through this Messenger to do the thing that was necessary? I am somewhat of a musician Myself, as well as an inventor. However, I do not have to use a brush in My artistic work.

Therefore, realize, Dear Ones, that you stand in the open doorway of all the Perfection there is. Isn't it worth any effort? Oh, there is no such thing as "sacrifice"; don't you see that? Whatever you discard of the outer world is a *release* instead of a sacrifice of any kind. Is there anything in human creation that would be a sacrifice for you to let go of?

Well, I think we have had quite a long visit this morning.

Question: Doesn't the vibraharp bring balance in the three bodies—balance the energy and the whole vibratory action of the three bodies?

Saint Germain: Now, let Me suggest that if you would play the "Song of the Islands" on that instrument, you would no doubt produce some very amazing results.

Question: How about having someone play it while you are working?

Saint Germain: Marvelous.

Question: How about making a transcription of the "Song of the Islands" on the vibraharp? Wouldn't that carry a very wonderful attunement over the air?

Saint Germain: Very! I want you all, if you will, to be so firm against all outer human suggestion, that when you have an inspiration—of course, be sure that the Inner Impulse is coming from your "Presence"; then quietly go ahead and carry it out, and see whether it works out, because that is the way you attune yourself for whatever your "Presence," through the Higher Mental Body, might want to do.

You will find from time to time more and more marvelous things will come forth by which to hold the attunement of the people; but oh, there is so much! We cannot bring it all forth at once.

There are certain instruments, perhaps five or seven, which will produce some extraordinary results. I won't say anything further about it; but when you get that certain combination together, it will produce a result on an audience that will be very, very remarkable. These are modern musical instruments.

Question: Do you refer to the combination of the instruments in the orchestration?

Saint Germain: Yes. You see, the outer world has believed that certain instruments in orchestration are essential. You will find you will be able to change those with other combinations, producing far greater results than has so far seemed to be authority for that in the outer world.

If you were to hear the flute We have, you would hardly be able to distinguish it from the human voice.

Question: Is that made of amber or a special material?

Saint Germain: A substance of Our own composition.

Question: Is that the same substance the harps are made of?

Saint Germain: Quite similar to what the violins are made of.

Question: Could the substance of jewels be used?

Saint Germain: That is being done. You will remember I said to you, the harp and the violin were made of a substance similar to mother-of-pearl; then can you for a moment imagine the exquisite tone of the vibratory action from that which is the purity of a pearl!

You see, jewels are the most perfect substance in the vibratory action of that color; so, if substance was drawn forth into the production of instruments representing that color, naturally your perfect tone production would be there. We have an instrument of far greater perfection than that one which I brought from Arabia for Mrs. Rayborn, that produces within three minutes a perfect attunement of the body, the physical structure. When the time comes that We can bring that forth, We will do so; but We will keep the instrument from the visibility of the audience because, of course, the human inclination the minute something comes forth is to try to imitate it; and that could not be permitted, because they would probably produce the exact opposite effect. Then in some of these things the curiosity of mankind will reach its peak to hear something which they are not permitted to see.

Question: Could not a record be made and played over the public address system? Would that do it?

Saint Germain: Yes; but remember, in the reproduction of a thing you are bound to lose some of its perfection. When a thing is produced from an individual through the instrument—I mean in the perfection of the attunement of the "Presence"—you produce a certain result. In other words, you set forth causes that produce the exact result, while to produce that through a machine means you have lost some of the effect.

Of course, now I am referring to these instruments we are just discussing that come forth of this perfect substance; for really, the substance is perfect and produces perfect vibratory action for a given result. That is not known in the outer world so far.

Question: Could we presume to think perhaps there will be a collection of instruments come forth —for instance, the substance of the blue sapphire, that when one will harmonize with the tonal effects of that color, will actually be in the same vibratory rate?

Saint Germain: Not only will it produce the exact quality of that Perfection, but it will produce the color visible in the atmosphere and give the vibratory combination with it. Sound and color will become one, and one will produce the other.

Can you imagine the effects for a few moments of, say, seven instruments, each one representing a jewel producing that perfect quality which would produce its perfect color? Can you imagine that effect upon a group of mankind for thirty minutes? Then don't you see how it would be impossible for a destructive vibratory action to ever act within the compass of the walls in which this was produced.

For instance, you take a building like the Shrine Auditorium—you would find you would qualify the walls of the building as a fixed focus of this vibratory action. It would not go outside those walls, but would produce that Perfection within them. That is how We hold within a certain compass a certain vibratory action; then the full power of that would be held within the radiance of that building and within the radiance of the bodies that were within it. Therefore, you would produce exact results in every one of those bodies, because that would have no human resistance. It makes no difference what previously had been acting in that human body. When that vibration went forth, the other would be unable to act; and probably when it was finished, it would not be there to act. Therefore, you see how We are coming at very, very definite action that produces always the same mathematical results, because then outer conditions will not interfere with that vibratory action which is the power governing.

Question: How about using jewels for healing?

Saint Germain: You see, that would be the concentrated focus of this Power which we are speaking of. That would be—for the sake of explanation, shall we say in case of emergency that would hold the powerful, concentrated focus.

Now then, please understand this; then we must stop: In this vibratory action of which we are speaking, it would be impossible, no matter what the vibratory action had previously been within that human form, to produce a discordant thing there within it. This is the point I want you to get and hold in your mind. Therefore, it is not a matter of how much attunement that physical body has in itself, but *this would compel the attunement and sustain it.* Now we are getting at the Demand of the Cosmic Light. You see? That is coming back into Perfection, which the Golden Age represents.

Now, let us go one more step. In all governmental offices, in all governmental requirements your amplifiers would be there in the room—where the vibratory action and tone color which would produce the harmonious results, could be released into that room from a given center at any time. Then don't you see how it would be impossible for injustice, imperfection, and selfishness to find action. Don't you see how then will come, not only with the effort of the individual, but through so-called mechanical means—of course step by step, far beyond our present state, that will produce the exact result for any given purpose.

For instance, suppose one was to stand forth and give a discourse upon a given subject. Well, corresponding with this, the vibratory action and tone color would make the comprehension complete within individuals who were listening. You see how far-reaching it is? Through this Inner Activity of Our Radiation, which is producing a similar effect in a lesser degree because of interference of human qualities—yet this would obviate the interference of any human quality because it could not act then.

Question: Are these jewels and musical instruments You speak of, the true Inner Action of the Temples of Healing, the Temples of Light and Music?

Saint Germain: This is going considerably beyond what has been utilized heretofore. Well, this will be quite similar to what is in use on Venus at this time. Now then, you will understand why Venus sent forth her assistance to the Earth.

You will remember that an intimation was made that seventy people should be prepared to go to the Teton. If seventy people were prepared to give absolute obedience and hold absolute harmony within their feeling world, they could govern every condition within the government of the United States—or any other government of the world, for that matter—by the projection of these Currents of Energy into a given environment. You see, that is how powerfully the Light would come into action.

Question: You would have ten of each color?

Saint Germain: That would probably be varied by the requirements. But you see in the seventy-thousand-year civilization why there were two governing each outer manifestation—because this similar vibratory action was created without the instruments. Now for instance, in the Globes of Unfed Light which I drew forth for the lighting of the building which was the capitol, you see, that Light contained the same Action of which we are speaking now. It held the Radiance so powerfully within the room that no inharmony would manifest within that Radiance. Therefore, that was not nearly to the point where we are just speaking of now; but still, it did a tremendous work at that time in holding the harmony for the requirement.

I thank you, each one, for that great harmony, happiness, and attention; and may this ever remain a Sacred Moment in your lives henceforth. May this discussion release into outer manifestation the Glory of all which we have discussed, and give you the incentive to hold such harmony within the feelings that these great wondrous things may come forth.

I thank you, and Our Blessings from all of the Great Ones enfold you always. Lotus and Betty, you will find a great calm harmony taking possession of your atomic structures that will make it worlds easier for all that your Hearts wish to do. Please accept that in Its Fullness, that Its Action may quickly take place so that you have time for some recreation. I thank you.

CHAPTER XIII

September 7, 1938

Oakland, California

I greet you, Beloved Ones, in the Name, Love, Wisdom, and Power of your "Mighty I AM Presence." I am just come from Europe, and could you see the far-reaching power of indirect deceit and treachery that lurks on every hand!

I say to you, Beloved Ones, if any of you let yourself be used by anything that is deceitful or treacherous, you can just expect the full descent of that destruction upon yourself. I warn you now as never before. When people do as they are doing in Europe, they have no more consideration for honor or purity or promises.

If it were not for the love of the people for the Messengers, I tell you, there simply would be no hope. It is really the hope of America today.

My Dear Ones, if anyone is not willing to give the simple obedience, that lets a force in that drives into the Student Body. Well, then they are responsible for what happens.

Question: If it drives into the Student Body, that

affects America.

Saint Germain: Now, please try to comprehend. If the Heart of your body were affected, would it not affect the whole body? Those people who think they have Heart trouble, usually their whole body is affected by it. The Heart is the center of your body, and when it stops beating, it is the end of the body. If you cannot hold honor, purity, loyalty, and absolute honesty within yourselves, well then, don't you see it is exactly the same as the human Heart—it affects the whole body of the Students. It is so curious that the Students do not grasp that the feeling world of all the body of Students is really one; and the discordant, treacherous feeling of one goes out and affects the whole body to some degree.

Question: That does not mean that just because one may fail, that would stop the progress of the rest in the Light, does it?

Saint Germain: Oh, no. That has nothing to do with the individuals, but it has so much to do with the accomplishment of the Students for America and her protection.

You see, there are so many vicious individuals that are pouring forth and making each one a target for their viciousness, and trying to force and impel suggestions upon each one to make them do the impure and wrong thing; and if you don't stand guard over it, it will make you do it. You do not realize the power of suggestion through the feeling.

The moment anybody gets irritated or peeved, they should keep still and not allow themselves to talk until they control themselves.

I do say to you, be so kind and considerate of each other. I tell you, if you criticize in your feelings and pour forth those feelings to each other for any reason at all—oh, it is so silly. I say to you, it is just so silly for anyone to feel critical to the other; and don't do anything that has any chance of disturbing the other.

Question: I know that after each Prompting You give us, if we could feel it with redoubled determination, one of these days we are going to get where we don't make any mistakes.

Saint Germain: Everyone has the perfect ability to give the obedience that is necessary.

Question: I firmly believe that. While maybe it has never been done on Earth before, but if people really want to, they can be perfect.

Saint Germain: Of course they can.

Question: I mean perfect instruments, in every sense of the word, even though they are not Ascended.

Saint Germain: There is no question about it in

the world.

Question: What good are any of us if we have to have a spiritual policeman?

Saint Germain: Exactly. I often see weeks ahead the thing that is going to drive at the Students, but I cannot give any more Promptings than I am.

Question: If everyone had obeyed the Promptings You have given, there would not be any trouble.

Saint Germain: No, but We can only keep on trying. But I must take the Messenger and go on with the Work when we get to Seattle. I may have to take him days and nights for a time, because he can do such tremendous things with Me in Europe right now; and We cannot begin this Work while he is in Class.

Question: If we were so prepared, could we go with You at night in Europe?

Saint Germain: Yes. You have been doing it in the Higher Mental Body. You Blessed Ones, if you could see the Work he and Lotus do during the time these bodies sleep, you would be the most astonished beings.

Two days before the opening of the Chicago Class the greatest Release of the Cosmic Light so far will be released; and I trust at that time to gather and be able to do for America all and far more than We have contemplated. As I see it now, We must build up that centralized Focus for the Release of the Light at Chicago and hold it sustained there.

I want to tell you, Dear Ones—and say this wherever you can put this forth, either to the Students or the parents—I tell you, this hitchhiking is the most dangerous thing young people ever encountered because it throws them into an element that is absolutely disastrous—because, if you knew the vileness that goes on among some of those hitchhikers, oh, it is indescribable. So many of our young men and some young women that were college graduates, because they did not have anything else to do, conceived that idea and began to run around over the country; and it was not six months until their whole lives were wrecked. I could point out to you a thousand of them today. They have just wrecked their lives through the vileness of the contact that comes through those who are timeworn hitchhikers—they come into such depravity there is no way to describe it.

You cannot quite comprehend how there are hundreds of instances where, if you as the focus forget to make the Call, then We just have to wait. That is so often the case when there are conditions to be handled. That means all the Students. If when something in their midst arises and they would instantly just leap into it, as it were, and *make the Call,* well, such release could come that would ofttimes stop the whole effect of a thing that might later occur from it.

Question: May I ask if that Current that passed through my body today was something very powerful for my freedom?

Saint Germain: Yes. Accept it as the great perfecting activity, because many times when you are just in the particular quiet attunement, then the Higher Mental Body will release that Power to do things that might otherwise require months.

I tell you, you do not realize what a Call at a certain time when you are in the proper attunement, will do for you. There isn't anything impossible in your Call to the "Presence." You have seen and known the experience of the Messengers, and that at an unexpected moment these Marvels are done. It is a natural Law of Life; and if one would not limit the "Presence" as to what It could do for them, it would be wonderful. But you see, mankind have been building this up; they have limited the "Presence." They do not know the "Presence"; but many of the Students do go right on with the same old feelings and desires, and of course it annuls the Call to the "Presence," at least to a very large degree.

Such great strides, such progress has been made with each one that you should feel the greatest encouragement in the world. I prompt you, every one of you, watch out! Stand guard when something, either from the mental or feeling world, tries to intrude and make you believe you are not progressing. Just hit it and annihilate it on the spot. If you allow that to get revolving, it is a dangerous thing.

I want to call to your notice another thing, because I mentioned in the Shrine Class that there was an attempt to hold that sleepy influence over the Class. It certainly requires wisdom when you are handling the human part of humanity; but that just shows the power of suggestion, and how they suggest those things to themselves.

Now, there really was not any definite projection here at the people to make them sleepy; but the thing they were trying to do was try to drive in irritation. But I did not let it touch the audience. Therefore, most of it was acting on them; but you see again that *you have to balance the outer activity with the Powers you are calling forth from the "Presence,"* because of the Application that you are calling forth. Many times It will not come through as long as the individual is temporarily too stubborn and vicious in the feeling, because it keeps repelling It; but the moment the individual gets calmed down, then It begins to take hold and act.

You have no idea what a powerful Repelling Force is in fierce Determination. That is how it is with everyone; and if the Students understood this when they make that Statement to all human creation, *"You have no power,"* good Heavens on earth, in a few days you could so charge your feeling world with the constant Outpouring of the "Presence" that there could not be a discordant thing touch your world. It is a tremendous opportunity.

Question: You mean to keep charging your world with that Statement all the time?

Saint Germain: Yes, and when you say to all human creation or the individual, *"You have no power,"* the very force with which you say that, is the impelling—well yes, we could say the "compelling" force that releases from the "Presence" that Almighty Power of Light which not only knows that that is true, but goes forth and charges your feeling world with that dynamic Repelling Force that would, in a short time, make it impossible for anything to intrude into your world.

You could keep charging your feeling world twice, or three times a day with the Perfection of the "Presence" and the Power of Light; and in a short time, it has to take on that Power that is absolutely pouring out like a river when you make yourself Invincible—but you cannot do it if you keep accepting human irritation and disturbance and critical feeling in your feeling world. You keep annulling it all the time.

It does not make any difference what somebody else does. Don't let it affect you. If they make a mistake, that is their business; they have to pay for it. Don't let anything get you irritated or disturbed. That is the greatest thing in the world. You see the Messenger has to do it. He should be the greatest Example on Earth to you. What he does, any of you can do.

You see, *the greatest thing in the world where you are drawn together for a definite, powerful purpose is to know that loving cooperation and the outpouring of blessing from one to another.* It is imperative, and is the greatest thing that can possibly be done to cooperate with the Great Law.

Question: Can you tell us anything about the lights that were seen in the northern sky?

Saint Germain: They were Cosmic Activities of great Power. By the way, the flashes you saw tonight were powerful charges through the atmosphere.

Question: Were they in answer to our Call?

Saint Germain: Yes. Tremendous, really! And there will be more and more answers to the Calls, I mean in the outer manifestation.

Question: Is it good to get out into a place where you can make the Calls in the open?

Saint Germain: It is very lovely. It gives you so much greater sense of release and expansion. It is not that you could not do the same thing anywhere; but still, the human qualification today gives you so much greater release and expansion through the Call. For instance, it is just like the time you were in Muir Woods when the Messengers were there. There was an enormous Release that day. It is because the feeling world of each one is more relaxed, and you are really giving your whole attention to the thing in hand. You see?

Question: Are Faith, Hope, and Charity coming closer into the outer?

Saint Germain: Yes. You see, as the Cosmic Light is releasing more and more of Its Power, It is calling forth many of these Great Beings who have not been brought within the Earth's atmosphere for a long, long period. It has been a long time since Faith, Hope, and Charity were personally within the Earth's atmosphere—the same as the Goddess of Peace and Cyclopea and various others, Arcturus, and all those who are coming forth. It is a long time since Cyclopea came forth. He only came once in a hundred years for a long period; but now as this advances, more and more are being called forth.

Right at this point, if you only realized how it—the Call of Life—brings those Great Beings forth to minister to the Earth. Now, if you realize that your Calls that you make are the full Power of the Call of Life for the quality or thing that you need, don't you see how there could not be a single thing of human creation or conditions in the Universe that could hold it from you? It would be impossible. You know, every one of your Calls is the Call of Life which has the full Power of Life to release what you are calling for; but of course, the intellect and the feeling do not accept that in the fullness. You think you accept it in the intellect, but you are not accepting the fullness of it in the feeling that gives the instantaneous release.

Question: Saint Germain, don't look at the watch. We don't want You to go.

Saint Germain: I shall have to go presently, because We have tremendous work to do in Europe in the next twelve or fourteen hours.

Question: May we go with You?

Saint Germain: Yes, you may. When you go to sleep tonight, if you will make the Call I will try to have you retain the memory of some of it; or if not, I will try to impress it on the Messenger.

Question: Can we all go?

Saint Germain: It only requires your Call.

Question: When we go out at night, do we earn our salt, or do You have to tie us to a post?

Saint Germain: I want to say, Beloved Ones, if you had seen the Service rendered a good many times just in the past year, you would be rejoiced beyond anything you have experienced. But I say again to you, Beloved Ones, whatever you do, don't let the human or anybody else, or yourself, suggest to you that you are not making progress. Watch out for that, good and strong! Watch it with all you have, anytime it comes up; for you are making amazing progress.

Donald Ballard: Will you give us a special Charge of Energy and a special Blessing during the time we are going to be away now, and we will make an absolute unceasing Call that our every activity in Los Angeles when we go back, and our entire trip east, is exactly according to the Divine Law in every respect.

Saint Germain: I appreciate that Don, with all My Heart, because the transformation is so great within you.

Question: We make the Call that not the slightest

thing happens in our world to distort the Law, and ask for Your Protection and Blessing.

Saint Germain: I thank you with all My Heart; and you certainly have It, and I will direct It through the Messenger. Will you all stand and receive the Blessing?

★ ★ ★

Note: Saint Germain then gave His Blessing to each one, directed through Mr. Ballard's hands—first on the forehead. Then He asked each one to reach forth their right hand, palm up, and He poured the Currents again through Mr. Ballard's hands. He stated that He had been hoping to do that for a long time, but it could never be done before. It only goes to show what the Great Law may do at any time.

Saint Germain then asked all to pour forth their love and blessings to Mama and those in Los Angeles who were there making transcriptions.

CHAPTER XIV

September 14, 1938

SEATTLE, WASHINGTON

How very great, Beloved Ones, is My Rejoicing in all that was accomplished in Los Angeles. I congratulate every one of you with all My Heart; and you, Precious Lotus, only as you see with the All-Seeing Eye within will you realize and know how tremendous was the release and the prevention of a confrontation gathering, which was consciously being attempted in Los Angeles.

I will appreciate it, Lotus, very much, if you will get all the sleep and rest possible during this Class. Don't do anything that does not have to be done, but get your rest; and I will charge the Current of Energy through these hands so that you come back into perfectly restful ease and action of your muscular system.

I tell you, please be at peace and rest. If it were not for the onrushing Cosmic Light, I would have very little hope of averting this calamity for mankind; but I know how great is the impelling Power of the Cosmic Light that is acting within the feeling world of mankind. Remember, seeing this in the beginning of this Work, and since the time was ready and these Mighty Decrees began to go forth into the mental and feeling world of mankind, the Cosmic Light has been the Power of Action. As It rushes forth, It will take Action in the mental and feeling world of mankind with a Power that has been or would be inconceivable without It.

I congratulate every one of you for your determination for self-control and the governing of yourselves and your feelings, to enable Me to do the things that can be done. I tell you, Precious Ones, could you just believe Me or feel within yourself the Glory that stands just in front of you, there would not be anything in this world that would make you have an irritable feeling about anything or anybody. It is the most marvelous freedom, financial release, and opening of the Cosmic Light to each one of you; it is marvelous!

Dear Ones, can you believe Me—I ask you to just for the minute mentally check up on some of the things that have been accomplished during your Meetings. You only seem a few, but when you realize that this Call and the Power released releases Infinite Power into action to do these things, then you will see what it has meant. I know you are not making a fortune insofar as money goes, but you are making a fortune ten times as great as if all the wealth of the land were dumped into your lap to use. You are not only winning your own Freedom and Victory, but you are rendering a Service to America unparalleled, because every foot gained in the Activity is a permanently sustained Activity that can never go back, no matter what comes in the appearance world. Nothing can interfere with every step that has been gained in the Acknowledgment of the "Presence," whether it is for you individually or the Nation or the international activity. Won't you tonight, every one of you, try to feel the full import of that. Whether it is individually, or for the state or the Nation, or for international activity—everything gained is a permanent, eternally sustained thing. Why, it is so stupendous!

Sometimes when I look over the audience and see the few individuals who doubt and question, I just long to release a thunderbolt into their midst—not unkindly; but I mean, to shatter that human shell and reveal to them the great Truth which is present for their blessing, because in this day of the Final Goal of mankind it is a very different thing than anything that has ever been on Earth, because mankind is having to choose—being *compelled* to choose—whether they are going to serve the constructive or destructive forces. But that decision comes from within the Light of the individual—not a human choice. The Higher Mental Body, when It gets the expansion of the Light to a certain point, then It chooses; if it has expanded enough, then the choice is for the Light, and there is nothing that can change that once that decision is made. So, it is not always the individual who seems to have failed in the outer—because the Light may take hold and reverse that thing. You see, so much is possible today that never has been in the history of mankind, because the determined intent and reaching out to the Light is the decisive power.

You see, if I were to precipitate—for instance, give a glass of that Liquid to each one of you, and you drank it now tonight, your bodies in the morning would look almost like different human beings. I have been hoping I could do that, and still hope that that can come about; but I must have sufficient harmony maintained within the feeling of the individuals before that can be done.

Question: Harmony over a certain period?

Saint Germain: Yes, it must be over a long enough period so there would not be any reaction or discord within the body.

Question: Would that take out all discord, so to speak?

Saint Germain: If sufficient harmony had been maintained for a length of time, then if this were done, it would make one almost invincible against it by any outside projection, except their own feeling within. But the greatest Service I contend this will do for the Student is to make them practically invincible against outside suggestions.

As the radio work continues, you will find that the class of people drawn into this Work will be marvelous. They will be firm, kindly, unyielding in their determination to the Light, and they will take hold of things and from the beginning shut off this foolish human gossip. Then they will be able to go ahead in the marvelous way. But as long as they listen to or become a part of that kind of thing, it creates such turmoil in their feeling world they cannot be stabilized. That is why the Messenger urged them in the Shrine Class and since, not to listen to or become a part of those things, a wide-open prey for the thing the destructive forces want to pour in.

I tell you, you cannot take people by the hair and make them accept this Work. If they don't want to come in of their own volition, just let them go their own way. This sounds, again, perhaps ridiculous, but from Our standpoint it is so true. The true human relationship is where people are in harmony. If they are not in harmony, there is no relationship, you see. That is the truth from the highest standpoint, but mankind in general would think I was a terrible creature to say that thing. They would surely swear I was breaking up homes.

That accounts for the conditions that exist in the world, because mankind have become wholly ignorant of the real or true laws governing those things. But so long as the condition exists, you just have to make the best of it until something can be done to raise the consciousness and the feeling world of mankind into that which is wholly different; and of course, the Knowledge of the "Presence" is the only thing that could do it and sustain it.

Someday when I show you the records of mankind, you will marvel with Me that the sanity of mankind has been sustained. I tell you, the way they have with great determination gone exactly opposite to the Requirements of the Laws of Life—and of course, it gets them into a state of consciousness where any kind of depravity seems a perfectly natural thing, don't you see, because then they would not resist it.

Question: Is there always one planet in every System of Worlds wherein the people do disobey the Law of Life, or is this just a stream that is accumulated?

Saint Germain: No, every System has its own planet which is the wayward child; but of course the Earth is the densest, by far, of all that disobedience.

You take our present humanity today. Those who arise out of this through their Call to the "Presence," become a strength and power unknown to those who have not gone through it. It draws forth the utmost of the Strength, Purity, and Fullness of the Divinity within the individuals. That means they gain the full Mastery. That is why the Ascended Masters are such marvelous Beings, because They have gained that Mastery through rising out of human conditions and limitations; therefore They are the Attainment of the Perfection and full Mastery over the most destructive forces that are in the human octave.

For instance, let us take Ourselves: when We have won the Ascension through the human Calls, it gives Us—not just because of having reached that state, but it gives Us a Freedom, Determination, and unyielding Power over human qualities and destructive things that just is not describable in words. That is the reason why in these Classes We are able to pour forth a Radiance and Substance that is—well, if you saw from Our standpoint, it is the most marvelous thing you ever witnessed, especially since the beginning of the Shrine Class when this greater Activity was entered into. It is a marvelous thing.

Question: Does this Liquid Light-Substance act as if It dissolves the covering from the Points of Light?

Saint Germain: Yes, It does do that; but perhaps this would make it clearer: It rather eats up the imperfection that is there. I would suggest to everyone that you feel that Liquid Light envelop and enter into your kidneys, your bladder and reproductive organs at least twice a day for two or three minutes. Just feel that enter in and dissolve all impurity and imperfection. The kidneys need it in almost every person these days very much, because the kidneys of every human being have been constantly overloaded with substance that is so difficult for them to handle.

If you ladies will just visualize from the base of your brain area and all along the spine to the end of the spine—like a tube of Liquid Light feeding off into the body through the vertebrae and through those nerve channels, you would find a great relief from a tired spine, because in addition to your Call to the "Presence" to charge the energy, you will find It a Sustaining Power.

I do urge all of you that are doing work that requires your bending forward, to stop three or four or five times during the day for two or three minutes, and lie across the bed or some place where you reverse the position of the spine. Oh, you would get such relief and keep from getting into that spine tension, because I tell you, when you are typing or writing or playing where your head must necessarily lean forward—you in years past when you were doing other work outside, you did not continue these things long enough to get the pressure; but where you work for hours in almost one position, it almost locks the spine and the flow of the nerve energy, and that is the reason you find this tension. Many times by putting a pillow under the shoulders and just letting go and relaxing, and let yourself relax over that, sometimes it relaxes the whole system and lets the Currents of Energy flow. Then there is no tension or distress; but when you get under the pressure of work, many times you do not feel you have time to do it.

Question: Wouldn't it help to let the head hang over the edge of the bed?

Saint Germain: Yes, but that is not quite the point. It is between the shoulders where they need the relaxation more than the back. That is why I suggest a pillow or something that is soft that doesn't make a hard spot—something soft between the shoulders, because that is the place where the relaxation is needed. All people more or less lean forward in the natural activity, because most people droop in the shoulders if they do not watch themselves.

You will note the Messengers stand for hours in almost an immovable position. Well, there are few people who can do that; but that is because they stand absolutely straight with the spine and all the nerves flowing in equal balance. The audience marvels and marvels how they can stand almost three hours in one position. That is the reason, because it is the natural Current of Energy causing them to stand straight. It is a very wonderful thing. You don't have any sense of exhaustion; you could not have.

When people do not realize these things, the natural tendency of the human is to drop into a position where they seem to be most comfortable; yet by habit, they come into a position where they are most uncomfortable.

Oh, there are so many little things that are so helpful and vital, but people do not do them because they let the pressure of the moment make them feel they haven't time to do it; yet if they would take the time, it would make everything else so much easier.

Question: This Liquid Light You spoke of, is It similar to that Garment of Light-Substance from the Secret Love Star?

Saint Germain: That is more for clothing; but this Liquid Light is a Substance that enters right in—similar to what you would use in drinking a precipitated Liquid, although that is still more powerful. I will never forget the first precipitated Liquid that Mr. Livingston drank at Mr. Rayborn's home at the mine. His hair almost stood up. While it is a most peculiar sensation, I am frank to say, the first time you take a precipitated Liquid into the system there is no describing it. You just cannot describe it, because It goes right through the system like Liquid Fire. And of course, you know how quickly the blood circulates through the body; then you can know the speed this goes through the body. It is almost like an electrical force, but it is just an indescribable thing and the effect is something marvelous.

When I first discovered this, and that I could produce It, I almost hesitated to try It. But I tried It out on Myself first, and I thought, "If I survive, somebody else might." I shall never forget the sensation. I certainly gasped; but I just waited for the results, and they turned out to be very marvelous.

Mr. Ballard: Was that what was coming into my hand?

Saint Germain: Yes.

Mr. Ballard: Had I continued that, would It have come forth?

Saint Germain: Yes; but the need of the other work was paramount at the time, and was the reason you did not continue it.

Mr. Ballard: Should I try it again?

Saint Germain: Well, just follow the Inner promptings; but I would not urge it just now, until we get more of this protective work accomplished. All of these other things will follow after enough of this is done, so the Protection is assured.

Question: Shall I keep giving the Decrees powerfully in the Contemplation Groups like I did in Oakland?

Saint Germain: Oh, I think so. It is magnificent. If you saw from Our standpoint what is accomplished in those Groups, it is tremendous. I mean not only for them individually, but for the release of the Power that We can use. I tell you, they get into a powerful sincerity; and you have observed, of course, that it always comes into the exact same Power and Energy in every Contemplation Group. There is hardly any exception, because you are able to call It forth. I tell you it is a Service that is tremendous, not only for America, but for the things that it is doing for them individually—

because when they get into that vibratory action, they take hold and make clear Application, where they won't do it most of the time for themselves. They get into that great, firm determination, and it is marvelous.

Question: May I ask how near the Light was to being Self-luminous about Charles, Pearl, and myself when the Power began to surge? Was that coming to the point of Luminosity?

Saint Germain: Yes. Don't be surprised at any time if the Self-luminosity comes into the room, or comes about your bodies. Don't be startled or surprised in any way, because It might suddenly release, just like It did with this good Brother and David Lloyd. He did not dream of such a thing and did not know it could be done, but it was.

I tell you, this is the point: The love of the Students is getting so great, and the Call is so great—just like David Lloyd calling to the Messenger for the Service to be rendered him. He had gained that momentum, and when it released, it released him from a human element that kept the Power of the "Presence" from releasing Itself.

That is why I have impelled the Messenger to say in these recent Classes, *"Do not limit the 'Presence' as to what It can do for you"*—because it is so important at this time because there are thousands of the Students that are ready, at some enthusiastic and joyful moment when this great Power of the "Presence" might easily be released.

Do not each one of you feel this tremendous, great, calm Joy that is throbbing through the room? It is marvelous.

Now, I must take you back for just a moment to our point of discussion. When you consider the children that come into life under the conditions of life that most of them do—at least seventy-five percent are so-called accidents—then you see why Life is so beneficent in providing the protection, in providing the Currents of Life and Energy and sustaining Power that make really beautiful creatures out of individuals drawn into conditions where really they were not wanted; and yet the mass of mankind are in that position, through one cause or another. One time it is lack of finances; another it is not desiring to be bothered with children; another time it is something else—oh, various things. But these are conditions now that you all must understand and not be affected by the knowledge of them, but understand from the standpoint of Life and Its Manifestation—the magnificent, beneficent Presence and Power of Life—that It does for the human form such marvelous, marvelous things.

Now, I call your attention to this point: I have seen children born into a family of almost depravity, and in this child the Light is strong enough that it rises right out of the surrounding conditions and influences there, into a beneficent, marvelous being. You have seen that done repeatedly. Now look, all your great financiers today, almost without exception, are people who were practically orphans. They were turned out in the world, so to speak, to become newsboys or individuals who almost from babyhood stood on their own feet and, by that great determination through the privation that was their experience in childhood, they built up that determination which compelled Life to surround them with wealth.

Any determination that is held firm and unyielding will produce exactly the same effect, because it is the Power of Life acting. Now then, in the Understanding of the "Presence" as you have it today, there is not one of you that could not start right in and fix your determination upon a goal and not reach it within a comparatively short time, because the Light would be compelled to act. It is not a matter of choice of Life acting; but your determination and firm, unyielding desire draws It forth and causes It to act upon that objective. It is a magnificent thing. There is no thing in the world that any of you could not have that is perfect, good, and true, by directing the Power of Life to produce that.

Question: What will Life do with what you might call the derelicts? Will the Cosmic Cycle in the cataclysm cut the forces away from the Stream of the individual, and bring them back and let them go forward, or are they too depraved?

Saint Germain: No. You see, the Goddess of Liberty gave to mankind one of the greatest things ever given to the Earth when in the Third Episode of Washington's Vision She has given forth: "If necessary, the Light of a Thousand Suns shall descend into the Earth and dissolve and consume all discord from the planet." That is the only hope of mankind.

Any human being on the face of the Earth who looks at that Chart and cannot see his Divine Origin is certainly in a bad shape, certainly is clothed with human creation that they cannot see through. Life should seek for greater Happiness, Beauty, and Perfection, rather than intentionally trying to lower itself. Wherever Life is manifesting through a human form, that is God Life.

The Discourse in the afternoon of the Ascension

Day at Oakland rendered a Service to the unions and to Mankind United, that will continue to expand until that thing is dissolved—because there were some of their people there, and they saw that it was only kindness that gave forth the truth to them; and they went out absolutely sure within themselves that that was the case. Therefore it has made them begin to think for themselves. There were two men there that were largely instrumental in the strike condition in San Francisco; and they have done some work, and they are awaiting further opportunity to reverse and change that whole thing—and I think through that, will bring about the annihilation of that whole thing and the setting free of those people. You never can tell from the outer standpoint, what individual might be in your audience, whose far-reaching powers and influence may change the whole state or whole city.

That is why We suggest—unless We see it is absolutely necessary—to hold your future work in the Classes as much on the constructive activity as possible, citing what the constructive does rather than calling their attention to the other things, because that work has been done to a large extent. We might occasionally refer to it. That will show these people then that there is nothing political, there is no belligerent feeling or thought back of the work being done in the correction of the conditions.

That is why sometimes it is necessary to become more dynamic and positive to release whatever it is with feeling, and call their attention to the fact that it is given forth with the greatest love and kindness, that mankind may understand.

Question: In Chicago, will we have to start in and do a lot of the fundamental work again, or shall we begin the Work where we are?

Saint Germain: I think I would give some fundamental work, because there are a lot of the people, even among the Students, who do not understand clearly; and I think it would be well, for the first two days, to explain many of the fundamentals. Then when you come back the next time you can perhaps use less of it.

You would be surprised, I tell you, how Students of three years, in the unusual vibratory action in the room, take hold and grasp points they have heard twenty times; yet they suddenly awaken to the full import and their comprehension of it. So, there is no chance of getting away wholly from fundamentals, because as long as new people are coming in all the time, they must have a certain amount of it. But most of that is given in the explanation of the Chart.

There is nothing in the world that stands as the living proof to the people as to why this Great Law is true, as the explanation of the Chart showing the reason why it is true—because without that, a great many will take it as a supposition; but if they pay attention when the explanation is given—why these truths are—then they see it. But you must realize too, that through the early training and the dictation of the Discourses and all you have had, that only a very small part of it has really been given out, because there has not been time to do it. But those first few in Chicago had the opportunity when it was given forth; still they did not grasp it then.

May I cite to your attention two things: Mankind listen without attention. I mean by that, that if you are listening to something and your mind revolves on something else, you are listening without attention and you do not comprehend what is being said. That is the reason why so many repetitions are necessary. The great majority of people sitting in an audience are listening apparently, individually; yet their mind is off thinking about their own affairs, problems, or some condition that exists—instead of just dismissing everything for that hour or two and giving the whole attention to the consideration of what is being said. That is the reason people do not comprehend, but you just have to be patient and keep on until they grasp it more and more.

I think we will try to arrange it and have each Class a large seventeen-day Class, because as the protection is given, then it will give time to give more explanation of these things; and as the vibratory action rises, the people will comprehend more rapidly.

Question: It gives ten days' preparation and seven days' absorption.

Saint Germain: I think by the time you have finished in Chicago it will really give seven days' preparation and ten days' absorption. That is what I hope to bring it to. Then you will see some real comprehension, and they will enter into the comprehension and Application with a power that is dynamic. A few individuals have done that; but the majority seem unable to, because just as soon as they begin to go back into the radiation and face their problems, they begin to accept that involuntarily instead of standing firm against it.

Question: Will You help us with the radio in Washington and see if we cannot get it in that Class?

Saint Germain: You just have to be a little patient there. Things are working out far better than it looks at present. A lot of Inner work has to be done there, and a lot is being done by individuals. There was an attempt there to try to shut off your Work, but they have not succeeded at all. As you keep pouring in the Currents of Light—I mean by the greater focus of the Class twice a year, then the Light Rays between times—you will find that whole thing goes down, and there will be just as marvelous acceptance there as anywhere; but the regulations are quite a lot different there than in other places in the United States.

I want to say to the Messengers and the Staff, I thank each one for your assistance and the great, tremendous Work which was done in Europe the night before last and last night. You were all there giving tremendous assistance.

Now then, Blessed Ones, sleep with the greatest peace and rest and refreshing activity you have ever known, tonight. Feel the full Charge of the Liquid Light acting within your feeling world and bodies, dissolving every imperfection that is there; and remember, My Hand is in yours to your Eternal Victory—unless you should think I am too whimsical to keep it there.

Lotus, have the Messenger direct the Currents through your spine tonight so you get the full, complete relaxation and rest as much as you can during the Class.

Question: Shall I have the vibraharp in the room here or at the Class?

Saint Germain: I think it would be better here, because then you get the benefit of it before retiring; but I think by the time you sleep in the Radiation tonight, you will find you are quite refreshed. I trust all of you can say to Me in the morning, "I have had the greatest night's sleep in my memory!"

Do you know that this is always a very great delight and rejoicing to Me as well as yourselves. It never can be a one-sided affair, you know. I give to you, and you give to Me, and we all give back to Life.

Good night, Blessed Ones, with all the Love of My Heart and the fullness of My Call to your "Presence of Life," to release and bring into Almighty Action Its Mighty Perfection now, and bless you with every good thing and the Limitless Power of your Light. Good night.

CHAPTER XV

December 17, 1938

Los Angeles, California

I greet you, Beloved Ones, in the fullness of your Life, in the fullness of My Enfolding Love that is finding Its Mighty Radiance in your feeling worlds.

How deeply I congratulate you on your willing obedience. Keep on, Beloved Ones, in the great Victory of your Light. All are gaining so rapidly in the Victory of that great, great Light. Do not let human qualities have any action. I cannot tell you—words are inadequate to convey to you My Gratitude for all the obedience that is being given and what it means to you, what it means to the whole world.

Do you quite realize that in the Victory of each one, how this means the Victory of America, then the world? I do not mean by that to cause you to feel undue responsibility; but I do want you to realize how much depends upon the harmony of this Focus, the obedience of this Focus.

We are rapidly coming to the Final Goal of the Victory of the Light. Of course, We do not recognize such a thing as failure. The Victory of the Light in America, to Me, is assured! The full outpicturing of that depends largely upon the staunch stand of the Student Body.

This attempt to throw over the Student Body financial fear is the last throe of the human destructive forces; and the financial fear, owing to the conditions that exist in the government and the industrial activities, is not so far governed. It is making a strong attempt to act through the Students; but I trust before the Shrine Class is half finished that We will have been able to dispose of that fear, and especially over this locality.

I wish the Law of your Being for a moment permitted Me to show each one of you individually your achievement since the Chicago Class. It is tremendous! Hold that sustained; and whatever confronts you individually, please do not let your feelings become aroused or disturbed in any manner whatsoever, because you are at the point now where the outpicturing of this Perfection will begin to take Its Dominion and Action.

But, My Dear Ones, do you realize what it means? You here in the Heart Center or Focus are steadily and surely like a mighty avalanche moving down the mountain! Hold steady to that Power and Focus of the Light and, you Blessed Ones, let nothing in the world turn you aside from this Service; for it means a goal you cannot in the slightest comprehend. It all seems so natural to you, I know; and sometimes you feel like you are not doing so much, and sometimes like more and more was being piled upon you to do; but still is the Great, Great Law working out.

Will you try for a few moments to comprehend with Me what it means and how it is that you are here. How is it that out of all the millions of people you have been chosen to become the Student Body? Think of it! If it were not that the Light within each one of you made it possible, do you think you would be here? That should be sufficient to give you Invincible Strength and Determination to silence every quality of your human, to compel its obedience to the Law under any and all circumstances. I feel so sure that not one of you will have any great difficulty in the future in absolutely holding complete self-control and mastery of yourselves.

Do you know that humanity is like a great group of children? If you saw a group of children at play in the street and a vicious avalanche of destruction was bearing down upon them and you could stop that, wouldn't you do it? So today, you are in a position to hold the balance of Light by obedience and harmony maintained in the feelings—to the degree that it is stopping the avalanche of destruction bearing down upon the Children of America. And as you would save that group of children in the street, so may you save the Children of America. It is so great, so far-reaching that it is impossible for you to even conceive of a sacrifice upon the human part in whatever is required for that accomplishment.

You do not realize, Beloved Ones, how the whole world is looking upon you as ideals. You have no idea how so many are watching to see whether or not you will yield to things of the outer world. That is why today, My Love is so great for you; My Gratitude so great for your accepting My Humble Efforts to prompt and correct, that you might be that Victory—oh, not only for yourselves, but in this great need of today.

The world is like lost children not knowing which way to turn. Only those who are anchored in this Light have any stabilization, and you cannot imagine what the feeling is that goes through the feeling world of those millions of individuals. For instance, may I again call your attention to Italy, Russia, and Germany. Germany in its catapulting into this recent condition is perhaps a greater illustration than any other spot. Could you know the fear, the agony, the distress that surges daily through those blessed people—the majority who are so good and mean so well—just because those individuals have been seized upon and made insane.

Do you realize, My Beloved Ones, that only an Ascended Being could endure what it is to look upon people in the position of Italy, Germany, Russia, Japan, and China today. Could you not see and understand the causes back of it, no one could endure it; and yet, there beating each Heart is the Power of Light and Freedom, forgotten so completely.

How fortunate you are that your Light was sufficient to draw you into this Eternal Focus, which with your greater and greater obedience will mean the Ascension of every one of you. There is not one thing now can prevent It except yourselves! Even though the shell of your body remains, still would It be accomplished—the greatest privilege ever bestowed upon mankind.

You have not quite realized your position, your Service that you are rendering which has made all of this possible; but do you not realize the great Truth the Messengers have said to you so many times: "When you have served the Light enough, then the Light turns and serves you"—the greatest feat of accomplishment ever in the history of the Earth. That is what has made the success of all

Students of all ages—that they were able and strong enough to stand in their Service to the Light until the Light turned and began to serve them.

Do you realize today how grateful each one of you should be to be free, how grateful the Students throughout America and the world should be in this Understanding! To have had these points clarified for them and stand not only in their connection with the Presence of Life, but their conscious Application of how to hold such obedience of the outer until the fullness of that Power takes Its Dominion naturally through the human form—it is so magnificent!

Tremendous Power is being drawn for this coming Class; and the greatest things ever accomplished will be accomplished for the Student Body during this Class—not only those here, but those who are not able to reach here.

Will every one of you make definite, powerful Calls twice a day for the limitless Release of the money supply required for this Work? If you will do that, I shall appreciate it; and wherever you can, disabuse people's minds that these Messengers are millionaires. This has definitely been spread in order to try to cut down the gifts of the people; but We say to that, "It has no power," and that goes into every influence sent forth to do that.

Within the hour it has been made possible for Me to render you a Service which I have longed to do, and may you rejoice with Me in that achievement. In the days to come you will really and truly know what it means to have strong and powerful Friends, and the world has really never known what Friends mean until they have the Ascended Master Friends.

In the period in which your attention was upon the sustaining of Life in the body, it was a vastly different thing than now; for now, the whole world's attention, practically, has been called to the Ascension. You see, there is no Final Goal in sustaining Life in the body. It is a tremendous power of achievement. I mean, you go from one vast achievement to another; but in the accumulation of that very great Wisdom and Power, still you are not Free. *Only in the Ascension do you become wholly Free Beings!*

Therefore, at this period when the Goal of mankind, the Ascension, has been permitted to be given to mankind, and now the new Dispensation—can you believe Me when I say to you that in the beginning of this Work six years ago, such a thing as this new Dispensation was not even conceived of? That has all been drawn forth from within the Great Silence by the unfolding Activity, since you first began giving out this Work in Chicago.

You see how these things come about, by the vast

and tremendous Call of mankind! I tell you frankly, the people that are secretly making these Calls, even just having heard the transcriptions—it is amazing. That is why the Great Ones seeing this—and when the Goddess of Light joined the Goddess of Liberty in this tremendous Work, and in the intercession of the Central Focus of all Light, Power, Wisdom, and Energy to this System—then from within that Great Light were revealed these possibilities which cannot be revealed and are not revealed until the time approaches for mankind's release, which can only come through the Calls of mankind.

Do you realize that only since the close of the Second Golden Age have such Calls ever been made from the body of humanity as are being made today? In your busy lives I realize you have little time to think of those things, but still it is true; and oh, what a Service to render this Service to the Light!

Question: Saint Germain, does the Law of our Life Streams permit, or would You take out of each of us all desire and capacity to ever want anything for ourselves, or want our own way about anything? Why should any of us who have spent centuries building all kinds of vicious conditions—God knows what, and we don't want to know—ever again want our own way?

Saint Germain: I would qualify it in this way: I would take out the desire for individual achievement.

Question: I do not mean that. I mean the dissolving of the human that cannot have its way.

Saint Germain: The desire for the human to have its way, I think, would cover that entire feeling, because that desire is taken out; and that is what We are really proceeding to do today in raising your desire world into the Command of the Higher Mental Body. It means ere long the complete dissolving of the human desires, which would include one's desire for having his own human way because—now each one, please remember this, since this point has been brought up—the moment you feel resistance one to the other, it means that that is a human quality acting. And it is up to the individual who feels that, to stop it immediately and know that its business is to perfect its own world and to be harmonious and cooperate, each one with the other. That is imperative, because as the Light expands, the one who will not do that would be thrown out of the Light—not by any one's desire, but the very Light Itself would throw them out of the Heart Center by Its ever-intensifying activity of the Light. Therefore, in these promptings there is no reason why anyone should not govern it.

Question: When you realize every bit of unhappiness anybody ever experienced was caused by their wanting their own way—that was the thing I want taken out.

Saint Germain: Well, this today will assist tremendously in that; and I think everyone has been realizing more, more, and more not only the need, but the reason why this is necessary. To gratify human desires is an obstruction always to the freedom of the Light; but in the Service of the Light, to be harmonious and cooperative will cause the Light to bring about this which We have begun today.

I say this to you: if you cannot discuss a point happily and harmoniously, discontinue the discussion. Don't feel, anyone, that you are each other's keeper. The kindness and consideration of each other is absolutely imperative. You are dealing at this point with the Mightiest Law in the Universe; and each one has within them now the Power of Complete Achievement, but not if they judge each other.

There is one point I want to bring to your attention. My little pal has rendered gigantic service to America as Lafayette. You don't know the half of it yet. All I ask is that it may keep on. Your absolute self-control and obedience will allow the outpicturing of all that that service has meant. One of the reasons why the Great Law and why I have been very happy to provide for you financially at this time, is because of your great generosity to America, to Washington in that time of great need.

Donald Ballard: Saint Germain, notwithstanding, if there is any way I can give more service in balance for what I received, I wish it would come about.

Saint Germain: Just make your Call and the Great Power of Life will adjust all of that.

Tell Me, do each of you feel this tremendous glowing Circle that envelops you? You remember how at Chananda's Table this enveloped the heads of the individuals? This envelops your whole bodies in an even far greater Power than that which was in Chananda's Home. So, please feel that you stand and rest within the Great, Great Sanctuary of Life.

These meetings—no words could describe what it means to each of you! But to have that complete love and blessing, one to the other, would so quickly bring into action and reveal certain things that would make you rejoice forevermore; but as long as there is one who does not give that, then all must wait until that one gives the needed obedience. So, each one please see their own responsibility to the rest of the Student Body; and know that each one's entire business is the harmonizing and perfecting of your own feeling world and your self-control.

I wonder if you quite realize that the Messengers request not one thing that is not My Desire, My Wish, that will enable Me to do more and more for each one of you. I want to so much, and how long I have waited for this time! Sometimes, when from the appearance world it seemed it would be impossible, still, in knowing the appearance world had no power, has it arisen. Won't you do the same thing, each one in *your own* feeling world; and every time it feels resistance to the other, simply say, "Be silent!" and see that it is silent—all human feelings. You will be so happy, and it will give Me the opportunity to do so much more which I have longed to do but could not. Today has been started that which I trust will help each one of you so quickly to attain complete self-control and mastery, and give completely into the Hands of your Higher Mental Body your entire desire world.

This has made Me so happy today; and do you realize, Precious Ones, that we are entering into this Shrine Class in the greatest harmony ever experienced so far! So, let this help all to enter into this great Activity with absolute, complete harmony in everyone, and give the opportunity for Life, the Great Ones, to do to the fullest capacity everything They wish during this Class.

Beloved Ones, Our Work is accomplished for today. May I offer you My Thanks, My Praise, My Gratitude forever; and may you feel that freedom, that mastery, that self-control which is yours today and forever. Be alert! Stand guard over your feeling world! The moment it tries to arouse any kind of resistance or disturbance, conquer it; and remember that firmness toward human qualities does not mean humanly dominating anyone.

Oh, My Dear Ones, what a tremendous thing to be a part of drawing mankind's attention to the "Mighty I AM," the Presence of Life. Oh, think of it! That alone would be the greatest Service on Earth.

I thank you for your love, your presence; and may all that has been started into action today continue its mighty work until you are lifted in the Arms of your "Presence," unto your Eternal Freedom. Thank you and bless you, each one.

By the way, Najah wishes Me to convey Her Love and Blessings to the Messengers and the Staff. You have no idea the Ascended Masters' great Love when They see you arise in the Strength of your

"Presence" and render this Service—never is there such rejoicing in the Octaves of Light as to see those on Earth nearing their Victory and Freedom.

Thank you, and good afternoon.

Unveiled Mysteries . . . . **Volume 1**
By Godfré Ray King

The Magic Presence . . . . **Volume 2**
By Godfré Ray King

The "I AM" Discourses . . . . **Volume 3**
By the Ascended Master Saint Germain

Ascended Master Instruction . . . . **Volume 4**
By the Ascended Master Saint Germain

"I AM" Adorations and Affirmations;
"I AM" Decrees . . . . **Volume 5**
By Chanera

Ascended Master Discourses . . . . **Volume 6**
By the Ascended Masters

Ascended Master Light . . . . **Volume 7**
By the Great Cosmic Beings

The "I AM" Discourses . . . . **Volume 8**
By the Great Divine Director

The "I AM" Discourses . . . . **Volume 9**
By the Great Cosmic Being, Beloved Mighty Victory

The "I AM" Discourses . . . . **Volume 10**
By Beloved David Lloyd

The "I AM" Discourses . . . . **Volume 11**
By the Ascended Master Saint Germain to the Minute Men

The "I AM" Discourses . . . . **Volume 12**
By the Ascended Master Youth, Beloved Bob

Beloved Saint Germain's Talks . . . . **Volume 13**
By the Ascended Master Saint Germain

The "I AM" Discourses . . . . **Volume 14**
By the Seven Mighty Elohim

The Ascended Masters Speak on Angels . . . . **Volume 15**
By the Ascended Masters

Archangel Michael
Speaks on the Angelic Host . . . . **Volume 16**
By Archangel Michael *(to be released in 2001)*

The "I AM" Discourses . . . . **Volume 17**
By Beloved Master Jesus The Christ